I have said on many occasions th(
and girl into Scouting, it would do r
else we could do to restore our c
have been so fundameni

GEORGE VOII
Senator from ⌐

*In this day and age it is a relief and an inspiration to
read the uplifting, true-life stories in* The Scouting Way.
*It has truly brought us all together throughout the world
and proven Scouting and Guiding are a true brother
and sisterhood worldwide.*

ED BRIERLEY
Group Commissioner, Langley Scouting, BC Canada

*One of my greatest pleasures is communicating with young
people, both in and out of the military, about the
importance of character and values.*

GENERAL HENRY H. SHELTON
Former Chairman of the Joint Chiefs of Staff

You are a great help and an inspiration to your communities.

JULIA CHILD
Chef, Author, TV Host

*I commend you on your decision to write a book about
Scouting and the wonderful values it teaches.*

JOHN F. SMITH
Chairman of the Board and CEO, General Motors

I think what you are doing with
The Scouting Way *is WONDERFUL!!*

DAVE BURRIER
Asst. Scoutmaster, Hamilton, OH

*I am a Webelos Den Leader, den leader coach and Cub Scout
trainer. I am sooooo happy to have found* Scouting Way.
*I will use these stories in my den and pass them on to others.
It is so important for kids to have good role models,
so thank you for helping to provide that.*

JANIS TIPTON-KING
Boy Scout Leader, San Francisco, CA

I am confident that the virtues presented in your book will provide citizens with the valuable knowledge that is gained through Scouting programs.

STROM THURMOND
Senator from South Carolina

What a great thing you have done…I applaud your effort with this one more great way to influence kids in a positive way.

SANDI MARASCO
Boy Scouts District Executive, Temecula, CA

We need our youth to be more cognizant of their special place in our society and the demands the future has in store for them.

HALE IRWIN
Golfer

Your newsletter stories are inspiring. Thank you for your effort in making the world a better place!

CYNDI OLSEN
Boy Scouts, Antioch, CA

My primary contribution to it is to say that along with family and church, Scouting was terribly important in shaping my standards and values.

ADMIRAL STANSFIELD TURNER
U.S. Navy (retired)
Former Director of the CIA

Thank you for a great idea! Now in my 10th year of Scouting, second troop (my first troop moved on to college), I find the girls love stories all the way through. I will be using inspirational stories that my girls can relate to at my troop meetings for sure.

JOAN LOWE
Girl Scout Leader, Havertown, PA

I have great respect for Scouting and the values it embodies.

M. DOUGLAS IVESTER
Former Chairman of the Board and CEO,
The Coca-Cola Company

I applaud both of you for serving as Scout leaders and for helping young people to develop the skills needed to fulfill their potential. You will no doubt have a lasting impact on their lives.

JAMES B. HUNT, JR.
Governor of North Carolina

Thank you for sharing your creation with me. The hard work of you, your wife, and all others that helped in making the newsletter a success will inspire many Scouters and Scouters to be. I congratulate and commend you for this Good Turn. I will share this with my colleagues and fellow Scouters.

SONYA HERMANSON
Boy Scouts, Baltimore, MD

I salute your project.

CHARLTON HESTON
Actor

I think this helps boys and parents realize that Scouting DOES and WILL make a difference in their sons' lives, even though they may not see it as it is happening.

KAREN BUCHANAN
Cubmaster, Greenwood, SC

Thanks so much for your wonderful efforts for the youth of America!

DEB MORROW
Boy Scouts, Murphysboro, MO

As a Cubmaster and Asst. Scoutmaster and father of three boys, I often feel like I'm in a one man battle against those who would rather have our sons grow up to be "politically-correct" than "morally-correct."

It's great to see organizations like yours that bring the values of Scouting to the forefront and give people the help they need to spread the positive impact that Scouting has on our youth.

TOM LAWRENCE
Cubmaster, Union Township, NJ

THE
SCOUTING
WAY

A Daily Guide to Living
with Scout Values

Sandra & Jeff Schwartz

Published by The Scouting Way
PO Box 73302
San Clemente, CA 92673-0111 U.S.A.
orders@ScoutingWay.com
www.ScoutingWay.com

ISBN 0-9715398-0-4
Copyright ©2001 Jeff Schwartz

Third Printing
September, 2002

The Scouting Way is not an official publication of, nor endorsed by, the Boy Scouts of America, Girl Scouts of the United States of America, or any other organization.

Recycled

Book Design by Peri Poloni, Knockout Design
www.knockoutbooks.com

DEDICATION

The Scouting Way is dedicated to our son, Greg, and daughter, Lauren, who have kept us active in Scouts and challenged us to lead and be true to the Scout Laws.

CONTENTS

ACKNOWLEDGEMENTS

The Scouting Way is the result of a long journey and the contributions of many people. To say thank you, we offer the following tributes:

An Outstanding Service Award to the authors who took the time and effort to contribute their stories, whether they became part of the book or not. It is your stories that really bring *The Scouting Way* to life.

A Scout cheer to all the Scouts and adults of Boy Scout Troop 737, in San Clemente, California, for the great times and memories, especially Scoutmasters Dave Vollebregt and Juan Luna. And, the rest of The Committee: Mary Brooks, Ross Deaner, Ruth Eastham, Katy Fingal, Warren Foersch, Tom and Lucienne Hamilton, Laura Luna, Ellen and Mark McDannel, Bob Mignogna, Jay Paxton, Mary Shawver, Chris Travis, and Pete and Lynn Van Nuys. Come on over, the brownies are ready!

A Firem'n Chit to Net and Paul Allen for restarting the troop.

A Scout salute to our first Scoutmaster, Dana Huff, of Troop 760. You were always there as a mentor even after we left the troop. Watch out for those Ghost Chickens in the Sky.

A "caw" to fellow Woodbadge Ravens.

A Potlatch for Girl Scout Troops 1818, 647, and 1329, and leaders Jane Freet, Leslie Lothers, and Jan Ortega. Also, San Clemente Service Unit 1 for the training and comaraderie.

A special *Scouting Way* patch to the Boy Scouts of America and Girl Scouts of the United States of America for offering such great programs which help teach our children Scouting values and offer us unique opportunities to bond with them.

Parents' pins for Sandra's parents, Pat and Tom Nickols, both of whom were Scout leaders, and Jeff's parents, Brina and Emerick Schwartz, who was his Cubmaster.

A walking staff to Greg and Lauren for letting us walk the Scouting path alongside them.

A Reading Merit Badge for our editors Stuart "the King of Commas" Tewksbury and Pat and Tom Nickols.

A Try-it to Peri Poloni of Knockout Design for her inspirational cover and interior design.

And, finally, a magical backpack to carry inspiration wherever they go to all the loyal *Scouting Way* newsletter readers, for their encouragement and helpful e-mails.

HOW TO USE THIS BOOK

Way: A method for doing something.
A road to travel on.

T*he Scouting Way* is both a code of conduct and a path through life. Like life itself, it is both mental and physical. It is what we do as well as how and why we do it.

As we'll see in the following pages, *The Scouting Way* leads to the top: to the summit of our profession or sport; the best relationships with our family, friends, and co-workers; our peak potential as human beings; and the pinnacle of satisfaction in our lives.

To begin our journey, please read everything before the *Days*. Then, jump to the day of the current month. For example, if today is the 5th of the month, start with Day 5.

Each day, read only that day's chapter. Each chapter introduces a value, offers a real-life story about the value, and several suggestions for how to practice it throughout your day. (For months with 31 days repeat the day whose value you need to work on most or one you missed from February).

Then, throughout the day, find at least one or two opportunities to practice that day's value (for Type "A" overachievers, make it three).

When you think of new ways to apply a value, specific to your lifestyle, jot them down on the blank lines at the end of that chapter. This will help you in future months.

The Scouting Way is designed to be repeated each month. So, when you finish this month, start over again! Each day, make life a little better by living *The Scouting Way*.

A journey of a thousand miles begins
with a single step.

CONFUCIUS

PREFACE

It was one of the greatest nights of our lives: our son Greg's Eagle Scout Court of Honor.

As Committee Chairman, Jeff had been part of several Eagle ceremonies but he had been so focused on the programs that he missed some of their meaning.

However, sitting in the audience that night and looking at it from the outside, with no responsibilities save those of proud parents, we were awed. The whole was truly far greater than the sum of its parts.

Many of us were Scouts as kids. And, although we may still be able to recite the Boy Scout Law or the Girl Scout Promise, when was the last time any of us reflected on what those words really mean?

For that matter, most current Scouts can rattle them off without thinking—and that's just how they do it—without thinking about what they are pledging to do.

As Scouters (adult Scout leaders), this was a constant source of frustration. So, the theme of Greg's Court of Honor was breaking the Scout Law and Oath down into individual rules and exploring their relevance to our daily lives.

As one Scout recited the formal text then another told us all what it meant to live by that code, the words came alive, blossoming with meaning. It was awe-inspiring and made us proud. Proud of our son and proud to have helped him and other boys achieve this goal.

It was reassuring just to confirm that, in spite of the reported deterioration of values all around us, some people still strive to be Trustworthy, Loyal, Helpful, and all the other values that we learn in Scouting.

Is this all a little corny? You bet. Does that diminish its importance? Not one bit.

That night we wanted to become Eagle Scouts, too. But we understood, with some sadness, that we couldn't, being well over the eighteen year-old limit.

Happily, a few minutes later we realized that while we couldn't earn the *rank* of Eagle Scout, we had it within our power to *live* by those values, no matter our age. All we would need to do would be to focus on being Trustworthy, Loyal, Helpful, Friendly, Courteous, Kind, and all the other Scout values, all at the same time, as we went through our day.

Regrettably, we had to admit that we couldn't. As important as these values are, we simply didn't have room in our mind to focus on all these goals and still run our business, manage our household, and meet our other obligations.

We returned our attention to the ceremony as the speaker talked about how unattainable the Eagle rank seemed to young Scouts. He spoke of the Eagle Mountain: how high and insurmountable it appeared—yet the Scout climbs it by putting one foot in front of the other and never giving up. And, the proverbial light bulb went on!

If we could break the process of learning to live like a Scout into small steps that even busy people like us could easily integrate into our everyday lives, we could reach our goal.

And right there, *The Scouting Way* began to take shape. Although we couldn't quit work and devote our lives to our quest, just by being a little Friendlier one day and finding a few ways to be Helpful another, we would begin living more like a Scout.

Helping people is important, rewarding work. The tough part, for many of us, is finding ways to do so. Teaching people to read in a third world country would be useful and enormously satisfying but the reality is that few of us will ever do it.

We have families who depend upon us and careers or schooling that we're in the middle of. But we can make the world a better place in small ways, each and every day.

Deep down, we all want to leave a positive mark on the world. *The Scouting Way* helps us identify core values, relates them to today's challenges, and offers an easy, non-intrusive way to integrate them into our lives.

Welcome to *The Scouting Way!*

Yours in Scouting

JEFF AND SANDRA SCHWARTZ

A MESSAGE FROM THE CHIEF OF NAVAL OPERATIONS

The Boy Scouts of America and the U.S. Navy have enjoyed a long and mutually beneficial relationship. For over 90 years, the Scouts have imbued future Naval Officers and Sailors with the values and leadership skills they needed to better serve their Navy and their Country.

In return, Sailors give back to the Scouts by serving as leaders, mentors, and examples of good citizenship to our Nation's youth.

As a proud Eagle Scout myself, I fully appreciate the importance of Scouting. I learned a great deal about myself as a Scout and how to work as a team member. Scouting also taught me the essence of good leadership.

I support the Boy Scouts of America and encourage my shipmates to do the same. Today's Scouts will become tomorrow's leaders, making service as a Scout Leader or volunteer a valuable way of contributing to a better future for us all.

JAY L. JOHNSON
Admiral, U.S. Navy
Chief of Naval Operations
Eagle Scout

ORIGINS OF
THE SCOUTING WAY

T he concept of a *code of conduct* dates back to the Greeks in the third century B.C., where young men took an oath to become citizens of Athens:

> *We will never bring disgrace on this, our city, by an act of dishonesty or cowardice.*

> *We will fight for the ideals and sacred things of the city both alone and with many.*

> *We will revere and obey the city's laws, and will do our best to incite a like reverence and respect in those above us who are prone to annul them or set them at naught.*

> *We will strive increasingly to quicken the public's sense of civic duty.*

> *Thus in all these ways we will transmit this city, not only not less, but greater, better, and more beautiful than it was transmitted to us.*

Later, in the Middle Ages, English knights lived by the Code of Chivalry. Lord Robert Baden-Powell, founder of the Scouting movement, cited this code in his seminal 1908 book, *Scouting for Boys by B-P*:

Be Always Ready, with your armour on, except when you are taking your rest at night.

Defend the poor, and help them that cannot defend themselves.

Do nothing to hurt or offend anyone else.

Be prepared to fight in the defence of England.

At whatever you are working, try to win honour and a name for honesty.

Never break your promise.

Maintain the honour of your country with your life.

Rather die honest than live shamelessly.

Chivalry requireth that youth should be trained to perform the most laborious and humble offices with cheerfulness and grace; and to do good unto others.

Several common threads run through both codes, including patriotism, bravery, respect for the rule of law, civic duty, honor, honesty, and leaving the world better for your having lived.

Baden-Powell used these codes as a model when he created the original Scout Law in the early twentieth century (as published in *Scouting for Boys*):

A Scout's Honour is to be Trusted.

A Scout is Loyal to the King, and to his officer, and to his country, and to his employers.

A Scout's Duty is to be Useful and to Help Others.

A Scout is a Friend to All, and a Brother to Every Other Scout, no matter to what Social Class the Other belongs.

A Scout is Courteous.

A Scout is a Friend to Animals.

A Scout Obeys Orders of his patrol leader or Scoutmaster without question.

A Scout Smiles and Whistles under all circumstances.

A Scout is Thrifty.

While the Boy Scouts and Girl Scouts (and Guides) in America and other countries have modified Baden-Powell's original laws, the fundamentals still remain, including: Trustworthy, Loyal, Helpful, Friendly, Appreciate Nature, Obedient, Cheerful, and Thrifty.

These, then, are the guideposts along *The Scouting Way.* If we can have a great time in life and become better people and citizens in the process, what more could we ask?

BE PREPARED

*Lord Robert Baden-Powell (known affectionately
as B-P) founded the Scouting movement. The Chief
Scout of the World talked about its origin in an
interview with the Listener magazine, in 1937.*

As a matter of fact, I didn't actually start the Boy Scout Movement, because the blooming thing started itself unseen.

It started in 1908—but the microbe of Scouting had got me long before that. When I was a boy at Charterhouse I got a lot of fun out of trapping rabbits in woods that were out of bounds. If and when I caught one, which was not often, I skinned him and cooked him and ate him—and lived.

In doing this I learned to creep silently, to know my way by landmarks, to note tracks and read their meaning, to use dry dead wood off trees and not off the ground for my fire, to make a tiny non-smoky fire such as would not give me away to prying masters; and if these came along I had my sod ready to extinguish the fire and hide the spot while I shinned up some ivy-clad tree where I could nestle unobserved above the line of sight of the average searcher.

Somewhere about 1893, I started teaching Scouting to young soldiers in my regiment. When these young fellows joined the Army they had learned reading, writing, and arithmetic in school but as a rule not much else.

They were nice lads and made very good parade soldiers, obeyed orders, kept themselves clean and smart and all that, but they had never been taught to be men, how to look after themselves, how to take responsibility, and so on. They had not had my chances of education outside the classroom.

They had been brought up in the herd at school, they were trained as a herd in the Army; they simply did as they were told and had no ideas or initiative of their own. In action they carried out orders, but if their officer was shot they were as helpless as a flock of sheep. Tell one of them to ride out alone with a message on a dark night and ten to one he would lose his way.

I wanted to make them feel that they were a match for any enemy, able to find their way by the stars or map, accustomed to notice all tracks and signs and to read their meaning, and able to fend for themselves away from regimental cooks and barracks.

I wanted them to have courage, from confidence in themselves and from a sense of duty; I wanted them to have knowledge of how to cook their own grub; in short, I wanted each man to be an efficient, all-round, reliable individual.

The scheme worked.

The men loved the training and Scouting became very popular in the regiment.

In 1899, I wrote a little book called *Aids to Scouting* for soldiers. It taught them observation, or how to track, and it taught them deduction, or how to read the information given by tracks.

As one instance of observation and deduction, I told how my bicycle had been stolen one night in India and how I tracked it down and discovered the thief. In the early dawn, I followed the track of the bike along a hard high road, not an easy thing to do if you look down on the road, but looking along the surface towards the sunrise one saw the track quite clearly ahead of one in the dew lying on the ground.

The thief had led a bike by hand because the front wheel was locked and he evidently didn't know how to free it. His footmarks alongside it were those of a soldier's boots, not a native's sandal. I observed that he passed the turning which led to the Cavalry Barracks, so I deduced that he was not a cavalryman; similarly he passed the road to the Infantry Barracks, but when he got to the Artillery road he turned up it and went into their Barracks.

So I had only to tell the Adjutant of the Artillery that I believed one of his men had possessed himself of a very nice looking bike with a locked fore-wheel, and in a very short time my bike was returned to me, having been found hidden under the bed of one of the men.

That was one incident of many in the book to show the value of observation and deduction. When we were besieged at Mafeking, in 1900, my Chief Staff Officer, Lord Edward Cecil, got together boys in the place and made them into a cadet corps for carrying orders and messages and acting as orderlies and so on, in place of the soldiers, who were thus released to go and strengthen the firing line.

We then made the discovery that boys, when trusted and relied on, were just as capable and reliable as men.

Also, from experience of the Boys' Brigade, I realised that men could be got voluntarily to sacrifice time and energy to training boys. Then my idea that Scouting could be educative was strengthened also, through the following incident.

General Lord Allenby was riding to his house after a field day when his little son shouted to him, "Father, I have shot you, you are not half a Scout. A Scout looks upward as well as around him—you never saw me."

There was the boy, sitting up in a tree overhead; but far above him, near the top of the tree, was his new governess. "What on earth are you doing up there?" cried the General.

"Oh, I am teaching him Scouting," she said. She had been trained at Miss Charlotte Mason's College for Teachers, and they had been using my book, *Aids to Scouting*, written for soldiers, as a textbook in the art of educating children.

Then in 1907, I, as a General, was inspecting 7,000 of the Boys' Brigade at Glasgow on its twentieth anniversary, and the founder, Sir William Smith, was very pleased because the total strength of his movement was 54,000. I agreed that it was a big number but added that if the training really appealed to boys there ought to be ten times that number.

"How would you make it appeal?" he asked.

"Well, look at the young fellows in the Cavalry, how they enjoy the game of Scouting, which makes them into real men and good soldiers."

"Could you rewrite *Aids to Scouting*," he wondered, "so that it would appeal to boys instead of to soldiers and make them into real men and good citizens?" So I did that.

But before writing the book I planned out the idea and then tested it. I got together some twenty boys of all sorts, some from Eton and Harrow, some from the East End of London, some country lads and some shop-lads, and I mixed them up like plums in a pudding to live together in camp. I wanted to see how far the idea would interest the different kinds of lads.

I told a friend what I was doing, and said that I wanted a quiet place, out of Press reporters and inquisitive people, where I could try the experiment; she offered me the use of her property—Brownsea Island in Dorsetshire. And there we set up camp for a fortnight. I had the late Major Maclaren and the present Sir Percy Everett to help me and we taught the boys camping, cooking, observation, deduction, woodcraft, chivalry, boatmanship, lifesaving, health, patriotism, and such things.

The results upon the boys in that short space of time taught me the possibilities which Scout training held for boys. So I at once set to work and wrote the handbook, *Scouting for Boys*, intending it to be useful to the existing boys' organisations such as Boys' Brigade, the Church Lads' Brigade, the Y.M.C.A., and others.

The book came out in fortnightly parts at 4d. a copy. Before many of the parts had been published I began to get letters from boys who had taken up the game for themselves, boys not belonging to the Boys' Brigade or any other association.

All the following year boys were writing to me telling me how they had started Patrols and Troops and had got men to come and act as their Scoutmasters. So we had to start a Headquarters office in a tiny room to deal with correspondence and supply equipment. I remember my Secretary wondering whether, if we laid in a stock of twelve Scout hats, we should be able to sell them all!

In that year, 1909, I arranged to have a meeting of the would-be Scouts at the Crystal Palace on a certain day. And when I got there, my wig, there were a lot of them. Rain was threatening, so we mustered them inside the Palace and arranged a March Past and counted them as they entered at one door and went out at the other.

There were 11,000 of them. 11,000 who had taken it up of their own accord! That is why I say that one didn't see the start: Scouting started itself.

Then, among the boys as they marched past, we found some groups of girls in Scout hats with staves and lanyards and haversacks, like the boys. "Who are you?" we said.

"Oh, we are the Girl Scouts."

"The devil you are!"

"No—Girl Scouts."

So I had eventually to write a book for them giving them the name of Guides to distinguish them from Scouts. And that is how the Girl Guides started—on their own—and they have gone on growing ever since.

Soon, we began to hear from the Oversea Dominions and Colonies that they were all taking up Scouting, and before long foreign countries too were translating *Scouting for Boys* and playing the game.

In 1912, I had to go on a tour through America explaining the movement in twenty-four states. And I went on to Canada, Australia, and South Africa, preaching Scouting where they had all started it, but wanted to know more about it.

It was wonderful. Lots of people, of course, took to criticising the rapid rise of what they called a mushroom growth, and prophesied that after the first excitement it would gradually decline and probably die in the fifth year.

The fifth year came, bringing the Great War, so the movement had every reason to die then, for most of the Scoutmasters and all the older Scouts left to join up in the Services. Of these, some 10,000 were killed. But the movement did not die. The boys were put on their mettle to carry on and do service for their country in the time of its need.

Our danger was that enemy spies in the country would try to upset our war preparations by blowing up railway bridges, cutting telegraph lines, and so on, and at once Scouts all over the country mounted guard to protect such communications by day and night. Others were used as orderlies and messengers in government offices to replace men sent to the Front.

The Admiralty asked if we could send Sea Scouts to take over the coastguard stations and so release the naval ratings there to return to active service with the fleet. Luckily we had prepared a big rally of Sea Scouts in the Isle of Wight for the Bank Holiday of August, 1914, and the Great War, you may remember, broke out on that date.

So we were able to send off detachments at once to take over all the coastguard stations, from John o'Groats to Land's End. These detachments were mainly patrols commanded by their own boy leaders. We had some 25,000 boys doing their duty during the course of the War. They did their work thundering well, and after the War was over received the thanks of the Admiralty and of the King for their services.

So, instead of dying, the movement showed its vitality; it rose to the occasion and since then has gone on growing in strength and usefulness.

We have now 1,011,923 British Scouts and 544,544 British Guides. In addition to these, some fifty-two countries have taken up Scouting and many also have Guides, so that altogether in the world there are now 2,812,000 Scouts and 1,304,107 Girl Guides.

It should be remembered, too, that behind these there are many millions more now grown-up in the different countries who have been in the fellowship of the Scouts and Guides. But what is more important than numbers is the fact that these Scouts and Guides of all countries have arrived at the stage of being on very friendly terms with one another.

The Pan-American Jamboree, in Washington this year, of 28,000 boys, followed by the World Jamboree in Holland of another 28,000 (which thirty-two countries attended, all at their own expense), shows the enthusiasm of the boys for making friends with other nations.

There is in the movement that spirit of happy good comradeship which cannot fail in bringing about what we all pray for—Goodwill and Peace in the world.

This interview is available online, at
www.dshearer.fsbusiness.co.uk/sctfiles/bp_talks.htm.

DAY 1

CHEERFUL

*Maintaining a positive outlook and looking for the
good in every situation. Full of joy or gladness.
Seeing the glass half-full rather than half-empty.*

S couts know that a Cheerful attitude makes life easier
both for us and those around us. In addition to the Scout
Law about Cheerfulness, other values such as Kindness,
Friendliness, and Doing a Good Turn Daily make us feel
better about ourselves and the world, leading to a more
Cheerful attitude.

Take a deep breath and ask yourself, "What is special and
wonderful around me this very minute?" (Remember the
fun you had as a child, finding shapes in the clouds?) Look
around and you will find it.

Few people have it all but none of us lacks *something* to
be Cheerful about. Scouts look at each new day as a new
opportunity to make a positive difference in the world.

As Space Shuttle Astronaut Tom Jones demonstrates
today, in his out-of-this-world story, life is 10% what happens
to us and 90% how we feel about it. Today, let's focus on the
positive aspects of our family, work, health, and finances.

CHEERFUL

In November 1996 I had the privilege of flying on space shuttle Columbia on mission STS-80. Tammy Jernigan and I had trained for a year to go outside Columbia on two spacewalks that would test construction techniques and tools for the building of the International Space Station.

Our preparations included over a hundred long hours spent underwater in our space suits, practicing our work in the best simulation of weightlessness we can create here on Earth. Both of us were ready and anxious to get outside the shuttle and do what we had practiced for so long.

On Thanksgiving Day we put on our suits and prepared to open the hatch that opened into the vacuum of space. It would be the first spacewalk for both of us. Our hearts were racing as Tammy moved to rotate the hatch handle and open the door to the harsh sunlight of Columbia's payload bay.

Incredibly, we could not move the handle to the fully open position. The hatch was jammed shut! We struggled for two hours in the vacuum of the airlock to wrestle that handle into the "open" position, with no luck. Mission control cancelled our spacewalk that day, and you can imagine the glum atmosphere at our Thanksgiving Dinner that night.

A couple of days later we abandoned all efforts to get the hatch open and cancelled the spacewalks as too risky for the rest of our science mission goals. I was crushed with disappointment for a few hours. Tammy felt equally down. All of our hard training had been wasted, and our taste of the great space outside our cozy spaceship was to be denied us.

Yet we were quickly able to bounce back from the disappointment. Why? I looked around me and tried to look at the big picture. I was in space, orbiting our beautiful planet, whose stunning vistas beckoned just beyond our windows.

I was working and living with four wonderful crewmates: talented individuals with a fantastic team spirit and a will to succeed in our other work. I had been blessed to grow up in America, where a small boy could dream about flying in space as a Cub Scout and one day have that dream come true.

So I took stock, and realized how much I had to be grateful for, and that literally overwhelmed my disappointment. I could no longer feel sorry for myself from any perspective. I was soon smiling my way through my workday.

More importantly, my cheerful response to our bad luck (a loose screw had jammed the gears in the hatch mechanism) helped my friends aboard Columbia snap back into a good mood, and they no longer had to be concerned about me or lingering effects on my performance.

Dealing with adversity and overcoming it mentally—skills I'd been taught on Scout camping trips and on the trail to Eagle—is one of our most valuable internal strengths. In exercising those skills again, I think I came to enjoy that trip aboard Columbia more than any of my other two space shuttle missions.

I came away proud of my resilience, and confident I could deal with challenges yet to be encountered.

TOM JONES
Astronaut, Space Shuttle Columbia
Eagle Scout

Dr. Thomas Jones graduated from the United States Air Force Academy and served on active duty in the Air Force for 6 years. As a NASA astronaut, he flew four space missions and logged over 52 days in space, including 3 space walks. For more information about Dr. Tom Jones, check out www.jsc.nasa.gov/Bios/htmlbios/jones.html.

BE CHEERFUL

Below are several suggestions for becoming more Cheerful plus blank lines to add your own, specific to your work or lifestyle. As you go through your day, look for opportunities to be Cheerful and check them off as you carry them out.

❑ Stop what you are doing, take a few deep breaths, and count 3 of your blessings.

❑ Subscribe to a humor mailing list on the Internet and share a joke or a pun.

❑ Make a game out of an unpleasant chore. Remember Mary Poppins' maxim, "A spoonful of sugar helps the medicine go down."

❑ Whistle or hum.

❑ Put on lighthearted music or play your favorite album (or CD).

❑ Remember a funny part from a favorite movie.

❑ Pull out an old photo album and reminisce.

❑ Practice making funny faces with your kids (or parents).

❑ Play with a puppy or kitten.

❑ Remember your favorite birthday as a child or your child's favorite birthday.

❑ Call an old friend and get nostalgic about the *Good Old Days*.

❑ Buy yourself flowers and give half of them to a friend.

❑ Look for the humor in a situation. Don't take life too seriously.

❑ Invoke the Five Year Rule: If it won't matter in five years, it doesn't matter now. In five years, will it matter that your child spilled the milk or broke a dish? Will the fight you are having with your spouse matter then? If not, let it go now and concentrate on what *will* matter in the future.

❑ Sing in the shower.

❑ When you feel flustered or angry, stop for a moment and readjust your attitude to a Cheerful, positive one.

❑ Wear a portable cassette, CD, or MP3 player while exercising or doing chores and listen to energizing music.

❑ Smile.

❑ Get a dog, cat, or other pet. Unconditional love is always a source of Cheerfulness.

❑ _____

❑ _____

❑ _____

❑ _____

❑ _____

I lamented that I had no shoes, until I met a man who had no feet.

AUTHOR UNKNOWN

DAY 2

PATRIOTISM

Loving and honoring one's country.

Patriotism is more than just flying the flag on holidays. It's being part of the United States of America*, the world's largest melting pot. Celebrate Patriotic holidays by embracing their meaning, not just as another day off.

The military and political leaders who contributed their time and stories to *The Scouting Way* are testament to the indivisible connection between Scouting and Patriotism.

It begins the moment a Scout puts on their uniform, which proudly displays the flag, continues through parades and ceremonies, acknowledgement of the responsibilities of citizenship, respect and proper handling of the flag, and never ends.

Patriotism transcends all organizations and cultural backgrounds. Whether we are Native-Americans, African-Americans, Asian-Americans, or of any other heritage, we are strongest when we unite as *Americans.*

Fortunately, few of us suffer for our Patriotism the way Senator John McCain reports in today's *Scouting Way* story. His account of Patriotism, Bravery, and Perseverance offers lessons for us all.

* *For* The Scouting Way *readers in other countries, please substitute your country's name and holidays.*

MIKE CHRISTIAN

L et me tell you what I think about our Pledge of Allegiance, our flag, and our country. I want to tell you a story about when I was a prisoner of war. I spent 5 years in the Hanoi Hilton. In the early years of our imprisonment, the North Vietnamese kept us in solitary confinement or two or three to a cell.

In 1971, the North Vietnamese moved us from these conditions of isolation into large rooms with as many as 30 to 40 men to a room. This was, as you can imagine, a wonderful change. And was a direct result of the efforts of millions of Americans, led by people like Nancy and Ronald Reagan, on behalf of a few hundred POWs, 10,000 miles from home.

One of the men moved into my cell was Mike Christian. Mike came from a small town near Selma, Alabama. He didn't wear a pair of shoes until he was thirteen years old. At seventeen, he enlisted in the U.S. Navy. He later earned a commission.

He became a Naval flying officer, and was shot down and captured in 1967. Mike had a keen and deep appreciation for the opportunities this country—and our military—provide for people who want to work and want to succeed.

The uniforms we wore in prison consisted of a blue short-sleeved shirt, trousers that looked like pajama trousers and rubber sandals that were made out of automobile tires. I recommend them highly; one pair lasted my entire stay.

As part of the change in treatment, the Vietnamese allowed some prisoners to receive packages from home. In some of these packages were handkerchiefs, scarves and other items of clothing. Mike got himself a piece of white cloth and a piece of red cloth and fashioned himself a bamboo needle. Over a period of a couple of months, he sewed the American flag on the inside of his shirt.

Every afternoon, before we had a bowl of soup, we would hang Mike's shirt on the wall of our cell, and say the Pledge of Allegiance. I know that saying the Pledge of Allegiance may not seem the most important or meaningful part of our day now, but I can assure you that—for those men in that stark prison cell—it was indeed the most important and meaningful event of our day.

One day, the Vietnamese searched our cell and discovered Mike's shirt with the flag sewn inside, and removed it. That evening they returned, opened the door of the cell, called for Mike Christian to come out, closed the door of the cell, and for the benefit of all of us, beat Mike Christian severely for the next couple of hours.

Then they opened the door of the cell and threw him back inside. He was not in good shape. We tried to comfort and take care of him as well as we could. The cell in which we lived had a concrete slab in the middle on which we slept. Four naked light bulbs in each corner of the room.

After things quieted down, I went to lie down to go to sleep. As I did, I happened to look in the corner of the room. Sitting there beneath that dim light bulb, with a piece of white cloth, a piece of red cloth, another shirt and his bamboo needle, was my friend, Mike Christian. Sitting there, with his eyes almost shut from his beating, making another American flag.

He was not making that flag because it made Mike Christian feel better. He was making that flag because he knew how important it was for us to be able to pledge our allegiance to our flag and country.

Duty, Honor, Country. We must never forget those thousands of Americans who, with their courage, with their sacrifice, and with their lives, made those words live for all of us.

JOHN MCCAIN
Senator from Arizona
Former POW

Upon graduating from the U.S. Naval Academy, John McCain became a naval aviator. During the Vietnam War, he was shot down and spent almost 6 years as a Prisoner of War. Captain McCain retired in 1981, having earned the Silver Star, Bronze Star, Legion of Merit, Purple Heart, and Distinguished Flying Cross.

The following year, Mr. McCain was elected to the U.S. House of Representatives. He served two terms as a Representative before being elected Senator, in 1985. For more information about Senator John McCain, visit www.senate.gov/~mccain/biography.htm.

SHOW YOUR SPIRIT

Here are some ideas for being Patriotic and space for you to add your own. Check off the ones you have done.

- ❑ Fly the flag every day.

- ❑ Educate yourself on the issues, prior to an election, to ensure that you are making the best choices.

- ❑ Vote, even in off-year elections.

- ❑ Stand tall for the Pledge of Allegiance. Say it proudly and loudly and think about what it means.

- ❑ Write your representative and share your views and concerns. This feedback helps them make better decisions.

- ❑ Discuss the political issues of the day with your children. They are the next generation of Patriots.

- ❑ Read a book about life in early America.

- ❑ Acknowledge holidays like Veteran's Day and Memorial Day by giving thanks to those who have risked or given their lives for our freedom. Talk about Patriotism with your kids and make sure they know you take it seriously. For ideas, visit www.Patriotism.org.

- ❑ Visit historic sites with your family and discuss the significance of events that happened there.

- ❑ Buy a Savings or War Bond.

- ❑ Play a game with your family (or by yourself) looking at a map of the U.S. with the states outlined, and trying to name each state.

❑ Stand and sing the National Anthem when it is played.

❑ Help out at a Veterans of Foreign Wars post or other veterans' facility.

❑ Purchase *Made in America* products.

❑ Go on vacation domestically rather than internationally —help out an establishment in your own country.

❑ Play an album or CD of John Philip Sousa marches. Play it loud and proud.

❑ Put a flag decal on your car or bike.

❑ Enjoy one of the large 4th of July fireworks spectaculars complete with Patriotic music, such as those in New York and Washington, D.C. If you cannot attend in person, watch it on television with your family.

❑ Wear red, white, and blue.

❑ _____

❑ _____

❑ _____

❑ _____

❑ _____

Every good citizen makes his country's honor his own and cherishes it not only as precious but as sacred.

He is willing to risk his life in its defense and is conscious that he gains protection while he gives it.

PRESIDENT ANDREW JACKSON

DAY 3

PERSEVERANCE

Sticking to an aim or purpose. Never giving up on what you set out to do. Persistence, in spite of obstacles, discouragement, or failure.

Most things worth having require hard work and commitment. We may not succeed every time, even with Perseverance, but we are assured of failing every time without it.

Failure is temporary. Michael Jordan, perhaps the greatest basketball player ever, was cut from his high school team. But instead of giving up, he worked harder and improved his game.

His Perseverance paid off when he not only made the team but led them to a state championship. Michael Jordan understood that, as Vince Lombardi said, "It doesn't matter how often you get knocked down. What matters is how often you get back up."

Scouting develops Perseverance by giving Scouts and leaders the tools, training, mentoring, and encouragement they need to keep going. Each day is a new opportunity to take what we've learned and try, try again.

Remember when you (or your child) learned to tie your shoelaces? At first, it seemed impossible. Then it was possible, but took a long time. Now, of course, you do it without thinking. Your Perseverance paid off!

As the saying goes, "Inch by inch life's a cinch, yard by yard it's kind of hard." Any task, be it homework, sales report, repair project, or attaining the next rank can seem overwhelming, at first.

But, Scouting teaches us that by breaking it into small steps, it is achievable. Take it day by day and we can climb the Eagle Mountain—or rebound to the top of our game as WNBA star Olympia Scott-Richardson recounts in today's adrenaline-pumping *Scouting Way* narrative.

THE DRIVE TO SCORE

When I was asked to write a story on scouting values, I immediately thought of the value of perseverance. There are many instances in my life when I had to persevere through challenges.

The best example happened only a few years ago in 1999. In my first off-season from the WNBA I was pregnant with my daughter, BreAzia. I gave birth to her on April 7, 1999. Training camp started on May 3rd. Although I gained 65 pounds and had less than one month's recovery time, I decided to return to my team the Utah Starzz.

Fortunately for me, my husband, Al Richardson, is very supportive of my basketball career, hence, he came with me so that I could make a comeback and have my daughter with me at the same time. If he had not done that, I would have had to take that season off. As a first-time mother, I would not have felt comfortable leaving my month-old daughter behind.

When I began training camp, I was still 50 pounds overweight. Most WNBA teams have very rigorous training camp schedules and the Utah Starzz were no exception.

We had two three-hour practices a day. I participated in both practices as well as lifted weights and ran an extra hour on the treadmill each day. The first week I was getting migraine headaches from the stress of working so hard while overweight. I also put myself on several different diets during that time.

Although I was working so hard, when the official season started I was placed on injured reserve. This meant that I was technically considered to be on maternity leave, although I was present in training camp, working very hard. On maternity leave, players receive only half of their salary, so now I had three reasons to get back in shape: losing weight; getting placed on the active roster; and getting my full salary.

Unfortunately the task was easier said than done. On top of all of the work I was doing every single day to lose weight and strengthen my body to its original state, I was also a first time mother.

My daughter, cute and precious as can be, had colic. This meant that often times after drinking her bottle of milk she would get gas and cry from being uncomfortable. Luckily she got over that once she was a month and a half old.

The other issue was that she had her days and nights mixed up until 2 1/2 months old. She ate and slept most of the day, and was awake and hungry all night long. This meant that on top of all of the workin g out I was doing, I was also suffering sleep deprivation so I could tend to my baby girl at night.

I persevered through the harsh conditions of my second WNBA training camp and I finally lost fifty pounds by July. I was placed back on the active roster and three weeks later, I was traded to the Detroit Shock.

Although it was very unexpected and I missed my team-mates and coaches in Utah, I was happy about the trade because I ended up on a play-off team. Detroit lost in the first round of the play-offs but the experience was still thrilling. I was unable to participate in the end of the season because my thumb was dislocated and I tore two ligaments.

The next season in Detroit, all of my perseverance and leadership was rewarded with being named captain of the team. Although I did not play as much as I wanted to, I still worked hard and believed in myself.

The next year, 2001, again, my hard work and perseverance were rewarded with another trade. This time I went to the Indiana Fever. I was the starting center for the team and I had my best WNBA season ever.

I am still working hard and sacrificing so that I may improve myself as a person and player every day. I am currently playing professional basketball in Eregli, Turkey, so that I may still take my game to the next level. Perseverance is a never-ending task.

Often times in our lives we must sacrifice, as I had to during my first season back from having a baby. I had to sacrifice my time and energy. I even had to sacrifice the time I wanted to spend with my husband and daughter. Sacrifices are often necessary when one is persevering towards a specific goal.

The thing that helped me in this time of struggle was that I had confidence in myself and I had a vision. I envisioned myself in great shape, playing better than I had before having my daughter. I told myself that "if it had to be, it was up to me!" That was my mantra I repeated to myself as I ran on the treadmill everyday. I motivated myself when there was no one else to do so.

When you are persevering, confidence and vision are a necessity. One must see the light at the end of the tunnel; envision the finish line so that they may have the strength to continue onward, enthusiastically. Remember that when you are working towards a goal you must be enthusiastic. I heard a great quote once: "Nothing great was ever accomplished without enthusiasm."

When you are running a race, you run it hard, you compete so you may win, this is also true in life. People who run hard, who are unrelenting in their journeys towards their goals, tend to succeed.

I tell this story for younger people to understand that many of their role models have had a very rough road in one time or another in their lives. Many people think that those who are famous or successful are lucky.

I tend to think like my sister, Tres Christian, who told me luck is when preparation meets opportunity. When things aren't going your way, or you are yet to be rewarded, you must persevere. Continue to work hard; preparing yourself for any opportunity that may arise. Preparation and perseverance go hand-in-hand.

Perseverance opens doors of opportunity; it is the key!

OLYMPIA SCOTT-RICHARDSON
#0, WNBA Indiana Fever

Olympia Scott-Richardson, also known as "Big O," was an All-American at Stanford University. In her 4 WNBA seasons, she has played with the Utah Starzz, Detroit Shock, and currently with the Indiana Fever.

For more information about Olympia Scott-Richardson, visit http://www.wnba.com/fever/olympia_impact.html.

Persevere Today

The following are a few techniques for Persevering and blanks for adding your own. Persevere in something today, and check it off.

❑ Return to a project or problem you had given up on and give it another try.

❑ Help a child memorize something by making flash cards and practicing with them. Or, make up word games to help them remember.

❑ Organize a project by creating and maintaining a list of things to do, including deadlines.

❑ Take a class or read a book to learn software you have been struggling with.

❑ Be patient when recovering from an injury. Full recovery takes time and you do not want to re-injure yourself.

❑ Renew your efforts to get healthy by exercising more and eating better. Create a chart or spreadsheet to track your workouts and nutrition.

❑ Tackle a job you have avoided doing.

❑ When you are stuck and not making headway, take a break and do something else for awhile. Sometimes, clearing your mind allows a less-traditional approach to pop into your head.

❑ Become proficient with a new musical instrument, sport, or hobby.

❑ Finish a degree program in college or get your GED if you never graduated high school.

❏ Break a bad habit. If you can't do it alone, get into a program that can help.

❏ Carve up a large, intimidating project up into small, achievable parts.

❏ Don't beat your head against a wall. If the whole project is held up because of one obstacle, get help in that area. You don't have to do it all on your own.

❏ Congratulate yourself on a small success.

❏ Re-evaluate your expectations. Economic conditions and other factors can influence the achievability of forecasts. It is more motivating to achieve a slightly lesser goal than to fail to achieve a greater one.

❏ _____

❏ _____

❏ _____

❏ _____

❏ _____

Nothing in the world can take the place of persistence.

Talent will not; nothing is more common than unsuccessful men with talent.

Genius will not; unrewarded genius is almost a proverb.

Education will not; the world is full of educated derelicts.

Persistence and determination alone are omnipotent.

PRESIDENT CALVIN COOLIDGE

DAY 4

FRIENDLY

Outgoing, showing interest in others.
Offering a smile and goodwill to people you meet.
Open to new friendships.

Being Friendly means giving a little bit of ourselves to people we encounter. It is a win-win proposition that brightens the day both for us and the person to whom we are Friendly. Friendly is a smile, a wave, or a hello. It's an attitude that makes life happier.

Imagine if every person who crosses our path looks us in the eye, smiles, and says, "Hello." Try it today—the smiles you'll get back will be wonderful.

Let's not forget the friends we already have and be wise enough to lean on them when we need help. Be sure to send birthday, anniversary, and holiday cards or e-mails. Keep the relationship alive.

Scouts are among the Friendliest people in the world. They know that the best way to have a friend is to be one. Remember the Girl Scout song: "Make new friends but keep the old. One is silver and the other gold."

Some terrific lessons about Friendliness, from author and political confidant Letitia Baldrige, await in her *Scouting Way* story.

MAKING FRIENDS

When the Baldrige family moved to Washington, D.C. a million years ago, it was January, and my older brothers and I had to enter a new school where we knew NO one. My father had been elected to Congress from the state of Nebraska.

I was so used to having many close friends, and here I was at the age of six, going into first grade in the middle of the year. All the kids knew one another. No one said hello to me. Big depression!

Mother said, "I know how to fix this. You give them a party they will never forget. You show them how to entertain and have fun." (It never entered my Mother's mind that a six year old was not old enough to know how to be a gracious hostess.)

My birthday was coming up, February 9th, so she invited my entire class to a very simple lunch on a Saturday. She found adorable invitations with flags all over them, and she wrote in each one that my birthday was being celebrated along with George Washington's and Abraham Lincoln's, both of which came soon after mine.

Each child received a little book about the Presidents, we had horns with flag bunting on them to blow. One of my father's staff dressed up as Washington, and another one as Lincoln, and they gave the children a delightful presidential history lesson about their time in office.

Instead of playing "Pin the tail on the donkey," we played "Pin the stars on the American flag." I remember the ice cream desserts—molds in the shape of cherry trees.

Thanks to my mother, my birthday party was a smashing success. All of the children invited me from then on to play with them. My mother taught me how to reach out to them, and they in turn reached out to me.

She taught me that you don't sit around feeling sorry for yourself when you're in a new, strange situation. You do something nice for all the people who don't know you. It works.

LETITIA BALDRIGE
Author
Former Chief of Staff to Jacqueline Kennedy

Letitia Baldrige has written numerous books on manners and entertaining. She served in the American embassies in Paris and Rome and was the first woman executive at Tiffany & Co.

Ms. Baldrige is best known as Jacqueline Kennedy's Chief of Staff during the administration of President John F. Kennedy. For more information about Letitia Baldrige's books and life, check out www.letitia.com.

BE FRIENDLY

Below are some fun ways to be Friendly today plus room to add your own for upcoming months. Check each one off as you try it.

❑ Send a newsy e-mail or letter and catch up with a friend.

❑ Say, "Hello" to people who cross your path.

❑ Call or write an old friend you haven't seen in years, maybe one with whom you had a falling-out. Things that seemed important back then, in a heated moment, may not be now.

❑ In summer, go through your holiday card list and send everyone a postcard.

❑ Introduce yourself to someone you would like to meet.

❑ Bake an extra pan of something fun and share it with a neighbor.

❑ Send your e-mail buddies notes, not just forwards.

❑ Have tea or coffee with a neighbor.

❑ Talk to the person next to you in line.

❑ Catch another driver's eye, smile, and nod, "Hello."

❑ Take time to chat with a store clerk or server in a restaurant.

❑ When you share your news with someone, remember to ask what's new with them.

❑ Strike up a conversation with the new kid in school or new person at your office.

❑ Memorize the names of 3 people you interact with every day.

❑ Play peek-a-boo with a child.

❑ Introduce yourself to a new neighbor. Tell them about your favorite local restaurants, dry cleaner, grocery store, Scout unit, and other providers we all need to find in a new area.

❑ Smile and wave at a child in another car—watch for a big smile and return wave.

❑ Answer the phone with a courteous "Hello" or other friendly greeting.

❑ Create or join your community Welcome Wagon.

❑ Introduce yourself to your child's teacher at Back to School night or their coach at a game.

❑ Stop and let your dog play with another dog when you are out walking.

❑ Ask a co-worker about their family.

❑ _____

❑ _____

❑ _____

❑ _____

You can make more friends in two months by becoming interested in other people than you can in two years by trying to get other people interested in you.

DALE CARNEGIE

DAY 5

VISION

*The power to perceive the future by imagination or
clear thinking. Insight into problem areas. Foresight
in anticipating and planning for the future.*

Scouting is terrific for developing Vision. Outings and
meetings require Scouts to decide what the activities
will be, forecast and procure the food and other materials
required, assign duties, and organize transportation.

Then, we get to see the results of our Vision and its
implementation. What problems did we not foresee? How
accurate were our estimates of time and materials? Best of all,
we can incorporate what we learn into plans for future events.
Scouts quickly learn that goals are of little use without a
realistic plan for achieving them.

Many of us have a Vision of what we want for our business
life, such as a raise or a promotion. We need to do the same
for the rest of our life. What do we want our life to be in the
future, and what must we do to make our Vision a reality?

In the following *Scouting Way* narrative, Douglas Ivestor,
former CEO of one of the world's most respected companies,
relates his Vision and how he made it a reality. So, remember
the Scout adage, "Plan your work and work your plan."

THE FORMULA FOR COCA-COLA

Over the course of my career, a number of principles have been important to me. These may not work for everybody, but in sharing a few with you, it's my hope that they will help stimulate your readers to develop principles that will be right for them.

The first two principles I would like to mention are about concentrating on your aspirations and your passion for your work. Several times in my life and my career, I have had to elevate my aspirations—I have had to change the way I think about achievement.

I grew up in a small Georgia town called New Holland. Everyone worked hard there, and we all had certain ideas about success. I was fortunate enough to reach one of those levels of success when I graduated from The University of Georgia.

I did not set out thinking that I would be the CEO of The Coca-Cola Company. I worked in a grocery store throughout high school and college.

One day, while still in high school, I helped a man with his groceries. He was driving a brand new Pontiac GTO—my dream car! I asked him what he did, and it turned out he was a CPA. Right then and there, I decided if that job made you successful enough to have a GTO, I would be an accountant! And I became a pretty good one.

When I graduated from college and started working, my idea of success changed again. And when I joined The Coca-Cola Company, my goals continued to evolve. Throughout my life, this has been one of my principles: always elevate your aspirations. Never let your memories be greater than your dreams.

Underneath that idea of aspirational thinking is having a passion for what you do. I am often asked about the role models I have. My role models are people who are good at what they do and are **passionate** about what they do.

A wonderful carpenter worked on my house once. He was a true artisan, and he **loved** what he did. He was passionate about **perfection** in his job...and passionate about his **job**. After I moved into the house, he called and asked if he could bring his father to see his work!

Watching him work, he really became one of my heroes. It wasn't **what** he did, but **how** he did it. He approached his work as his art. He approached it with a passion. Seeing him helped reinforce another principle of mine: always approach your work with passion.

A third principle I would like to tell you about involves developing good training habits, good habits to learn. Coming out of college, I worked for Ernst & Whinney, the accounting firm (now Ernst & Young).

I thought I was a big-time, big-city accountant—until they gave me the very unglamorous task of auditing small-town nursing homes across Georgia. This involved going into unfamiliar (sometimes hostile!) surroundings and getting information from operators who had a million things they would rather be doing than talking to some kid auditor. Each week, just as I would start to get a little comfortable, it was time to move on to the next town.

Sometimes I got discouraged. I thought, "I can't do this"; but, I did, and I learned something. What I learned—to my surprise—was how to get in, devise a plan, get people cooperating, get the work done, write the report and get out—all within 40 hours or less.

I devised a routine, and got really good at it, and then there came a day when my firm needed an auditor who could go into this account, get people working together, get the work done and get out. It was The Coca-Cola Company account.

I believe my capacity for routine and hard work, my passion for what I do, and my willingness to always elevate my aspirations helped position me for the role I hold today.

I am privileged to lead The Coca-Cola Company and the talented team of women and men who infuse Coca-Cola and all of our brands with energy, excitement and magic each and every day.

M. DOUGLAS IVESTER
Former Chairman of the Board and CEO, The Coca Cola Company

Within two years of joining The Coca-Cola Company, Douglas Ivester became the youngest vice president in the company's history. Worth Magazine named him as one of the top 50 CEO's. For additional information about Mr. Ivestor, see www.horatioalger.com/member/ive99.htm.

DEVELOPING VISION

Vision, like all other Scouting Way values, needs to be practiced. Here are some ideas for increasing your Vision. And, be sure to have the Vision to add your own.

❑ Imagine yourself five years from now: Where do you want to be living? What do you want to do for work? How would you like to spend your free time? Create a five-year plan to make it so.

❑ Create a very specific one-year plan with your five-year plan (created above) in mind.

❑ Bounce an idea off someone with very different views. You may come away with a valuable new perspective.

❑ Create or update your family budget.

❑ Join your local Chamber of Commerce or another business development group.

❑ Take an inventory of your knowledge and skills. Are they being put to their best use?

❑ Start or add to a retirement savings account.

❑ Call one of your customers and ask them how they see the future of your industry. What would make your product or service more useful for them?

❑ Create or review your Will.

❑ Define your educational goals (or help your child define theirs). What degree do you want to pursue in college? Where do you want to go to school?

❑ Create a personal Mission Statement.

❑ Read a book by a futurist writer, such as Stan Davis or Faith Popcorn.

❑ Subscribe to a new magazine, newspaper, or trade journal.

❑ Consider your retirement. Envision the life you would like to lead, then build the dream.

❑ Set your Internet home page to a news site such as www.CNN.com. Or, if your home page is set to a portal like Yahoo, add news to it.

❑ Daydream about the future and let your mind wander.

❑ Be a *mystery shopper.* Check out your competitors' products and ask salespeople which brands they recommend and why. Don't tell them who you work for.

❑ Start a college fund for each of your kids.

❑ Read a history book. Remember George Santayana's sage advice, "Those who cannot remember the past are condemned to repeat it."

❑ Become active in a trade association dedicated to improving your industry.

❑ _____

❑ _____

❑ _____

❑ _____

❑ _____

You see things; and you say, "Why?" But I dream things that never were; and I say, "Why not?"

GEORGE BERNARD SHAW

DAY 6

LEADERSHIP

*Willing to take charge, guiding self and others
toward a mutual goal. Leading the way. Directing
activities or operations.*

L eadership is articulating the group's Vision and guiding it toward the common goal. But, it's more than simply pointing in a direction and yelling, "Go!"

The difference between a *boss* and a *leader* is that we follow our bosses' instructions because we are paid to whereas we obey our leaders because we elect them and believe in them.

There are no bosses in Scouting, so Scouts and leaders learn to motivate their team, minimize disharmony among members, delegate authority, and accept responsibility for both success and failure.

They know that the best way to lead is by example. If a Patrol Leader wants his patrol to readily accept direction from him, he must gracefully accept directives from the troop's Senior Patrol Leader.

Leaders must be Brave to do what needs to be done, regardless of the risk or their fear. They must be Loyal and Trustworthy so that their followers can count on them to do the right thing, no matter what. They must possess the

Vision to guide the group toward its goal and the Perseverance to press on until the objective is met. Only with these, and other *Scouting Way* values, can leaders earn the respect they need to lead.

As Scouts, we would never ask anyone to do something that we wouldn't be willing to do, or have done, in that capacity. By being leaders ourselves, we instill Leadership in our children.

Whether it's a large or small job, Leadership is important. In fact, as we'll see in a history lesson from Scouter Gary Wilson, it can change the world.

PREPARED TO LEAD

When we talk about teaching boys to "Be Prepared" we often don't know what challenges they will have to face as adults. Sometimes those involve the fate of the nation and the entire world.

I was moved by a National Public Radio *Weekend Edition* interview with noted historian and author Stephen Ambrose on the opening of the National D-Day Museum, in New Orleans. Here's a quote from Dr. Ambrose:

"Hitler was wrong. When he declared war on the United States, he made a bet, and that was that his young men brought up in the Nazi Youth would always outfight those soft sons of democracy brought up in the Boy Scouts. Hitler was wrong and he lost that bet. The Boy Scouts proved to be far more capable of making war than the Nazi youth."

My dad, Charles Wilson, tells a similar story. A Boy Scout in the thirties, he was drafted in 1942 and selected for Officer Candidate School, primarily because the Colonel leading the selection board was impressed that he was an Eagle Scout.

As an Infantry platoon leader and Company Executive Officer in Italy, he subsequently earned the Combat Infantry Badge, two Bronze Stars, and the French Croix de Guerre. But he tells the value of teaching self-discipline and "being prepared" this way:

"If the Lieutenant of a German platoon were killed, often the Germans would just stay in place and wait for another officer to arrive and tell them what to do.

"In the American Army, some sergeant, corporal or even a PFC, would always step forward and keep the unit moving and in action.

"The resourcefulness of the individual soldier, many of whom were Scouts, was the primary advantage of the American army in World War II."

So when we teach Scouts to be self-disciplined, self-reliant and to be prepared for leadership, you don't know how valuable that might ultimately be. Perhaps some day the fate of the nation and democracy might depend on it.

GARY WILSON
Boy Scout Roundtable Commissioner
Central New Jersey Council, BSA

Gary Wilson was a Life Scout and served in the Air Force Reserve. He has been a Scouter for 20 years and his son, David, is an Eagle Scout. Gary's Dad was an Eagle Scout, a U.S. Army Captain during World War II, and Troop Committee Chairman of Gary's Boy Scout troop.

LEADING THE WAY

Below are various suggestions for developing Leadership and, of course, space to add more as you think of them. Lead the way, today.

❑ Volunteer for a committee or to handle a project for your troop, pack, school, work, or religious organization. You don't have to be *the* leader, there are lots of opportunities to be *a* leader.

❑ Organize a Neighborhood Watch program.

❑ Chair the Book Fair at your child's school or the cookie sale for your Scout unit.

❑ Arrange a CPR class for your Scout unit, family, or company.

❑ Be the cool head in an emergency situation.

❑ Help your children become successful leaders by giving them responsibility for planning a meal or outing. Respect their Leadership while helping them, subtly, to ensure they succeed.

❑ Organize a group at your office to exercise during lunch or get together for another activity.

❑ Attend a Leadership training program, either through Scouting (such as Woodbadge) or business.

❑ Delegate a task you would normally do yourself.

❑ Think of a way to improve your Scout unit, school, business, or community and lead a drive to implement your idea.

❑ Mentor someone.

❏ Create a business plan for a new business you would like to start.

❏ Plan a motivational, spirit and team-building event for your Scout unit, sports team, or company.

❏ Coach a youth sports team at a Boys and Girls Club or other youth center.

❏ Run for an elected office, at any level.

❏ Organize your neighbors to deliver meals for the family of a sick neighbor.

❏ Attend a tradeshow for your industry.

❏ Join a business organization to meet and exchange ideas with leaders of other companies. Or, attend Roundtable to learn from other Scout leaders.

❏ Start a club or team at your school or work.

❏ Consider a change in your career. By re-evaluating your progress and goals, you will either decide that a change is for the best or realize that you are already on the right path and be happier and more content with life. Either way, you are better off for the analysis.

❏ _____

❏ _____

❏ _____

❏ _____

Leadership: the art of getting someone else to do something you want done because he wants to do it.

PRESIDENT DWIGHT D. EISENHOWER

DAY 7

LIVE TODAY

*Living in the moment, not waiting for some future
occurrence to enjoy life. Be here now.*

The recent terrorist attacks on the World Trade Center
and Pentagon show how suddenly, and without
warning, life can be over. Any day can be our last, therefore
we must seize each one. We could lose a limb or our
eyesight, so let's take a walk or enjoy a sunset, today.

However, Living Today does not mean disregarding the
future. Scouting teaches us to Do Our Best and Appreciate
Nature every day but also to be Thrifty, have Vision, and Be
Prepared for the future.

Sometimes it's difficult to strike a proper balance between
working toward a future goal, such as a college degree or
retirement, and enjoying the moment now. Scouting bridges
that divide by making learning fun and interesting.

Scouts have the best of both worlds: they have fun and
enjoy small successes while building toward their future and
bigger goals. Scouts never need to wait to be happy. This
strategy applies to life outside Scouting, as well.

One man who has shown an amazing ability to enjoy and
laugh in spite of very depressing situations is Dr. "Patch"
Adams. His prescription, in today's *Scouting Way* narrative,
is worthy of our consideration.

DOCTOR'S ORDERS

The advice I would give to the young people of America is, the most revolutionary act you can commit in our society today is to be happy, that if you really want to change the world, then you be your own focus for celebration of life and let it be known, whatever it is that gives you that happiness. Then, pursue your dreams.

Really, fundamentally, at the very core of your being, be thankful you're alive, that you've got this opportunity with these molecules at this moment. Be thankful and be a celebrant. Be thankful that you are alive and then look around and see who else is at the party.

Once you do that, then I feel that the magic is that you feel connected to life, that you feel that you belong to life. As big as you dare believe it to be, you belong to it. Your way of saying thank you is to serve, to say, "Okay, I'm in the picture, what can I do?"

So you celebrate, and that's your way of taking from the world, and you give back to it by helping out where your skills are. And a fundamental core of all of this for me—I have been a professional clown for 30 years—is having fun doing it.

DR. HUNTER "PATCH" ADAMS
Founder of The Gesundheit Institute

Dr. Patch Adams has dedicated his life to the idea that "healing should be a loving human interchange, not a business transaction." He has been prescribing healthy doses of laughter to his patients for over thirty years.

The 1998 movie, Patch Adams (with Robin Willims), chronicles his life and his vision for The Gesundheit Institute. For more information about Dr. Patch Adams, see www.patchadams.org.

LIVE TODAY

Balancing the desire to Live Today with the need to plan for the future can be tricky, but one doesn't have to be at the expense of the other. Here are some ways to Live Today that won't cost you tomorrow. Enjoy today, it will never come again.

❑ As you run your errands, notice the beautiful day or the flowers blooming. Don't just race through your tasks.

❑ Burn that special candle you have been saving.

❑ Take a nap, preferably in a hammock.

❑ Break out those special linens or the dish you thought was too pretty to use, and enjoy them!

❑ Run through the sprinklers.

❑ Tell your spouse and children how special they are, today and every day.

❑ Play a board game with your whole family.

❑ Don't worry if your house is not perfect, invite friends over anyway.

❑ Take a family outing to the park. Play catch with a Frisbee or throw a ball for your dog.

❑ Give your child a piggy-back ride.

❑ Sit quietly for a few moments and concentrate on taking deep breaths.

❑ Mend a broken friendship or family relationship. You never know when you will lose the opportunity to do so.

❑ Sing in the rain or along with your car stereo.

❑ Take a break from work and go out to lunch with your spouse.

❑ Organize a family reunion.

❑ Give flowers to your spouse (or boyfriend or girlfriend).

❑ Stop what you are doing and give your kids or spouse your full attention when talking with them.

❑ Make a snow angel.

❑ Go fishing, roller-skating, or another activity you enjoyed as a child.

❑ _____

❑ _____

❑ _____

❑ _____

❑ _____

A Prayer for Today

This is the beginning of a new day.
God has given me this day to use as I will.
I can waste it…or use it for good,
But what I do today is important,
Because I am exchanging a day of my life for it.
When tomorrow comes, this day will be gone forever,
Leaving in its place something that I have traded for it.
I want it to be gain, and not loss,
Good and not evil,
Success and not failure,
In order that I shall not regret the price I have paid for it.

Author Unknown

DAY 8

GIVE BACK TO YOUR COMMUNITY

*Donating your time or money to benefit your
neighborhood or area.*

We are all members of numerous sub-communities: family, religion, neighborhood, Scouts, and school. Each is an extension of our home. By Giving Back to Our Community we make it the best place it can be.

Scouts Give Back to Their Community by cleaning up beaches and parks, collecting food and clothing for needy families, visiting senior centers, and in numerous other ways.

Such community service benefits not only the community at large but brings Scouts and Scouters closer to their neighbors and makes their neighborhoods more nurturing places for their families to live.

We can employ that same spirit with similar results, outside of Scouting, by organizing a company blood drive, raising funds for our local school, or sending a needy kid to summer camp.

In today's *Scouting Way* chronicle, New York Governor George Pataki recounts the Bravery, Persistence, and Helpfulness of his state's Air National Guard—in a daring adventure at the bottom of the world.

THE EXTRA MILE

Growing up in the Hudson River Valley in Upstate New York, my parents taught me at an early age the importance of hard work, but more importantly, the value of helping others.

I can still remember with fondness helping my mother, father and grandparents around the farm, picking vegetables, weeding under a hot sun, and stacking hay.

Despite the long hours my father put in on the farm, he found time to serve many years as a member of our local volunteer fire company. Dad always told me that being part of the community meant you had an obligation to contribute to its growth and well-being. I can remember many times the fire horn sounded and my father dropped whatever he was doing to run off to the firehouse to help our neighbors.

I have carried that lesson with me ever since. After graduation from Yale and Columbia Law School, I returned home to the family farm and the community where I had grown up. I wanted to give back to my friends and neighbors and soon moved into public service—first as mayor of the City of Peekskill, then in the New York State Legislature and now as Governor of the Empire State.

The notion of helping others and improving our communities—such a core value of Scouting—is what motivated me to public service. Each and every day, my Administration and the men and women who work so diligently on our behalf are making our State a better place to live, work and play.

Not a day goes by that I don't hear about some instance of State employees going the "extra mile" in helping someone in their time of need.

Take for example, the heroic rescue of a doctor in need of medical attention from the South Pole by members of the New York State Air National Guard in October 1999. The 109th Airlift Wing of the New York State Air National Guard has provided airlift support to the National Science Foundation's South Pole research program since 1988. In 1999, the New York Air National Guard unit assumed the responsibility of being the sole provider of airlift support to the South Pole program, taking over for the United States Navy.

Flights in support of the South Pole program usually begin in late October to early November, the start of the Antarctic spring season, when the less extreme conditions will permit safer flights.

However, a member of the Foundation's South Pole research team, Dr. Jerri Nielsen made a self-diagnosis of breast cancer. Her condition made an earlier flight necessary, a dangerous mission conducted in temperatures at the very threshold of the ski-equipped C-130's operational capacity.

On October 6, 1999, the 109th launched two aircraft from its upstate New York base in Schenectady to Christchurch, New Zealand. Two days after the planes' arrival at Christchurch, the crews attempted to launch two aircraft for McMurdo Station in Antarctica, but were unable to successfully launch until the third day due to high winds and blowing snow.

Extreme cold temperatures at the South Pole hampered the 109th from launching for more than 24 hours after their arrival at McMurdo. Finally, on Friday, October 15th, one of the aircraft set out for the South Pole.

Three hours after takeoff from McMurdo, it arrived as the temperatures had warmed to the required -50 degrees.

The aircraft landed at the limits of its operating ability. Less than 25 minutes after the crew's arrival, the aircraft was off with Dr. Nielson and prepared to begin the long journey to bring her back for the medical care she needed.

The New York National Guard 109th Airlift Wing completed this historic medical evacuation flight on October 16, 1999— marking what is believed to be the earliest flight to the South Pole in the history of mankind's exploration of Antarctica.

The flight crew endured life-threatening, arctic conditions and executed an extremely difficult and dangerous rescue mission to help a woman they had never met. Their actions embody the true spirit of New York. Their bravery, compassion and genuine commitment to helping others are a source of inspiration to all Americans.

It is that spirit of selflessness and devotion to service and helping others that we ought to recognize and encourage— and that is a key reason why I think Scouting is such an outstanding and worthwhile activity for young people.

I wholeheartedly support Scouting, the noble ideals and goals it embodies, and the fine example it sets for our young people. Each of them, who give of their time, energy and talents to dedicate themselves to Scouting, is to be commended.

GEORGE PATAKI
Governor of New York

George Pataki graduated from Yale University and Columbia Law School. He became the youngest Mayor in the history of Peekskill, New York (his hometown) and served in the state legislature for ten years before being elected the 53rd Governor of New York. For more information about Governor Pataki, see www.state.ny.us/governor/.

Governor Pataki's letter was written before September 11, 2001, which is why it doesn't mention the dedicated people who Gave Back to Their Community after the World Trade Center bombings.

GIVING BACK TO YOUR COMMUNITY

In addition to the suggestions below, write in more ways you can Give Back to Your Community, specific to your locale. Put a checkmark next to each one you complete.

❑ Become a Boy Scout or Girl Scout leader.

❑ Take a job in your children's school PTA.

❑ Join a local Kiwanis, Rotary, Lions, or other community service organization.

❑ Help out at a senior center.

❑ Tutor students in reading or another subject at a local elementary school.

❑ Gather your friends and neighbors and pitch in when your town has a clean-up day.

❑ Sponsor a local youth sports team.

❑ Offer your time to a public or school library.

❑ Purchase scrip to support your local school and shop, whenever possible, at stores which accept it.

❑ Carry your local police dispatch number and call if you see an accident.

❑ Get involved with National Youth Service Day by visiting www.ServeNet.org or www.YSA.org.

❑ When a child comes to your door selling something to raise money for a local school or Scout unit, support them. If you can't afford to buy, donate a couple of dollars to the cause.

❏ Give blood, it's the gift of life.

❏ Donate time at your local animal shelter, walking or playing with the animals.

❏ Contribute extra vegetables from your garden to a food bank in your area.

❏ Work at a voter registration booth, get out the vote!

❏ Find out which labels your local schools collect (like Campbell's soups or General Mills cereals) and collect them.

❏ Purchase something through a website which donates a portion of the purchase price back to your community, such as www.SchoolPop.com.

❏ Attend the Homecoming Parade for your local high school, even if you don't have students there. Cheer loudly!

❏ _____

❏ _____

❏ _____

❏ _____

❏ _____

And so, my fellow Americans, ask not what your country can do for you, ask what you can do for your country.

My fellow citizens of the world, ask not what America will do for you but what together we can do for the freedom of man.

PRESIDENT JOHN F. KENNEDY

DAY 9

HONEST

Truthful, straightforward, sincere.
Without hidden agenda.

Honesty is a cornerstone of any relationship and at the very heart of Scouting. Someone could be the most Courteous and Cheerful person in the world but if they are not Honest, it is all for naught.

When dealing with dishonest people, we are always on guard, looking for the lie, fearful of being manipulated. We waste our time checking everything out for ourselves. Such relationships have no future.

On the other hand, communication with Honest people, like Scouts, is easier, more efficient, and far more enjoyable.

However, Honest does not mean offensive. Scout leaders know that an Honest evaluation of someone's work should not be insulting or demeaning. That creates defensiveness and shifts the focus from improvement to dealing with a damaged ego.

Combining Honesty with other *Scouting Way* values such as Courtesy and Kindness delivers the best results.

The old cliché is still true, "Honesty is the best policy." The impression we make can last a lifetime, as football great Raymond Berry relates in a poignant story about his father.

A POUND OF HONESTY

My dad was a high school football coach in Paris, Texas for 35 years. In those days each team in our district was required to weigh each player on the team and submit these weights at the beginning of the season.

My dad just died 2 years ago at age 95. While attending his funeral I had the opportunity to see many of the players he coached in the 1930's, 40's, 50's and 60's. One of his players on his 1941-42 team told about his experience "weighing in" one year. His name was Jake Coker.

Jake was determined to get his weight to 140, at least. He told me he ate many bananas and drank a lot of water. At weigh in he weighed 139. Jake said he tried to talk dad into giving him the 140 figure, but to no avail. I realized as Jake told me that story (Jake is 75 years old) that the influence of my Dad's honesty had never left Jake's memory.

I thought to myself, "Who would ever have realized how a seemingly insignificant experience like that could have such a lasting effect on a young boy's life?" It is a reminder to all of us that we have the power to impact people—sometimes for a lifetime.

RAYMOND BERRY
Hall of Fame Football Player

Raymond Berry was drafted by the Baltimore Colts and helped win three NFL championships. As coach, he led the New England Patriots to their first Super Bowl appearance.

Mr. Berry is a member of the Pro Football Hall of Fame. For more details about Raymond Berry, check out www.lifesplaybook.com/hall/berry.html.

Practicing Honesty

Below are a few ways to practice Honesty and blank spaces for you to add your own. Today, be Honest—no matter what —and check off each way you do so.

❑ Tell the truth. If you find yourself tempted to lie your way out of a situation, don't give in. Tell the truth and deal with the consequences. Never put your integrity at risk.

❑ Stop at stop signs and yellow lights; don't roll through.

❑ Pay your bills on time.

❑ If you find money in the street, return it to the owner if possible. If not, donate it to charity.

❑ Don't engage in false flattery or modesty.

❑ If a cashier gives you too much change, return it. It's a great feeling.

❑ Be Honest regarding your taxes. Tax avoidance is legal but tax evasion is not.

❑ Don't take things that are not yours, even small items like a magazine from a doctor's office.

❑ Be yourself in a new relationship.

❑ Resist the urge to cheat on a test. Honesty may get you a lower grade but cheating earns you an automatic "F" in life.

❑ Charge fairly for your services, even when you could get away with gouging.

❑ Pay people fairly for their services, even if you don't have to.

❏ Repay a loan promptly. If you are unable to, be up-front about it: tell them in advance and offer a partial payment. Such good faith efforts work wonders for your relationship.

❏ Make sure that your sales or other forecast is reasonable and achievable.

❏ Be honest about what time you have to give and don't over-commit yourself. It is better to take on fewer jobs but do them well than to take on more but let people down.

❏ Refrain from exaggeration when telling a story.

❏ Be realistic and don't create false hopes. If you cannot afford a certain present for your child don't lead them to think they will receive it.

❏ _____

❏ _____

❏ _____

❏ _____

❏ _____

I have found that being honest is the best technique I can use.

Right up front, tell people what you're trying to accomplish and what you're willing to sacrifice to accomplish it.

LEE IACOCCA

DAY 10

BE PREPARED

*Making sure that the necessary materials are
available, along with a practiced plan to use them,
in readiness of a need.*

With *Be Prepared* as their motto, Preparedness is
infused into all aspects of Scouting. Scouts Prepare
for everything from meetings to outings to service projects.
And of course, they are Prepared for first aid and other
emergencies.

But, we all need to Be Prepared and not just for an
emergency. Students need to come to class having completed
their homework; parents need to Be Prepared, financially,
to provide food and shelter for their families; graduates
require skills to get a job; office workers rehearse their
presentations; and manufacturing companies must ensure
that all required materials are ready for processing.

To Be Prepared, Scouts always carry their 10 Essentials and
stay Prepared as those items change throughout their life:

Students: pen, pencil, notepaper, calculator, books, book
bag, folder, change for a phone call, band-aids, parents'
phone numbers.

Teenagers: pen, notepaper, insurance information, gas
money, flashlight, cell phone or change for a phone call,
paperclip, parents' phone numbers, keys, band-aids.

New parents: toy, baby wipes, cloth, bottle, diapers, pacifier, plastic bag, extra baby outfit, blanket, stuffed animal or doll.

Parents of youngsters: toy, baby wipes, crayons, paper, book, band-aids, snacks, sweatshirt, extra outfit, blanket.

Parents of teenagers: pen, notepaper, money, paperclip, pocketknife, change, flashlight, cell phone, band-aids, patience.

Adults: pen, notepaper, paperclip, pocketknife, flashlight, insurance information, credit or bank card, money, cell phone, band-aids.

The following *Scouting Way* story from Internet inventor Vint Cerf reminds us that while physical preparation is important, we must Be Prepared mentally, as well.

PREPARED FOR THE FUTURE

Although my Scouting career was rather brief (Cub Scouts), my father became an Eagle Scout. I cannot think of anything that he did later in life that gave him more satisfaction.

Scouting's motto, "Be Prepared" serves well for virtually all aspects of life. To be Prepared, one has to think ahead, has to be knowledgeable and alert to events taking place.

Some people seem to be lucky, but my experience suggests that luck is largely a question of being alert to opportunity and recognizing good opportunities when they present themselves.

To some degree, one can also make opportunities by remaining open to new ideas and thinking "out of the box."

Many of the technologies that have fueled the Internet's expansion have been out of the mainstream and in some cases even ridiculed.

My personal experience is that persistence has counted for a lot with regard to the Internet and it seems likely that persistence will work for many other aspects of our daily lives.

I have also found that taking the riskier choice of jobs and challenges often proves to be the better and more rewarding choice. I've turned jobs down out of concern for my inability to accomplish them, only to be talked into trying anyway and discovering enormous satisfaction when it has proven possible to accomplish the task despite my own fears.

VINT CERF
Sr. Vice President, Internet Architecture, WorldCom
ICANN Board of Directors

Vint Cerf is the co-designer of the TCP/IP protocol and, along with his partner, Robert E. Kahn, was awarded the U.S. National Medal of Technology for founding and developing the Internet. For more information, see www.worldcom.com/about_the_company/cerfs_up/.

"Be prepared".

BE PREPARED

The following are some ideas for Being Prepared. Think of others that address the challenges you face and implement them today. Check each one off as you carry it out.

❑ Plan all your meals for the week, including snacks, so you only have to go to the grocery store once.

❑ Be Prepared, at both home and office, for a natural disaster with food, water, cash, and a plan. A valuable source of information is www.RedCross.org/services/ disaster/beprepared/.

❑ Before you walk into your office, mentally walk through your day.

❑ Check the equipment for your presentation one more time. Verify that people you are counting on will be there, on time. Bring an extra disk, battery, or cord. If it is an Internet presentation, make sure a live connection is available.

❑ Put all your important papers into one secure spot so you can quickly gather them in an emergency.

❑ Make sure your children know how to reach you if they need you. Put a business card or paper with your phone numbers inside their backpack.

❑ Back up your computer. Be sure to store a backup at either another physical location or on the Internet, using a service such as www.FreeDrive.com, in case your home or office is damaged.

❑ Take out a Life Insurance policy.

❑ Create a family plan for fire or other emergency. Make sure everyone knows it by heart. Then, practice it.

❑ Put a few extras in your car's glove box: granola bar, matches, pocketknife, flare, napkins, and emergency phone numbers.

❑ Take a course in CPR.

❑ Seal warranties in a plastic bag and tape them under electronics equipment.

❑ Designate a family member in another town as a contact point in the event of a local disaster. Make sure everyone has their phone number memorized.

❑ Make sure you have at least two meals prepared in the freezer.

❑ Get a personal toll-free number from your phone company. Your kids will be able to reach you more easily in an emergency.

❑ Memorize your Social Security Number.

❑ Make sure your car or bike is in top running condition, especially the lights and brakes.

❑ Start a fitness program to stay in shape for any emergency.

❑ Make sure all your electrical outlets, near water, are protected with a Ground Fault Interrupter.

❑ _____

❑ _____

❑ _____

❑ _____

By failing to prepare, you are preparing to fail.

BENJAMIN FRANKLIN

DAY 11

BRAVE

Doing what you know is right, even when you are afraid. Not letting fear stop you.

Scouts know that Bravery is not the absence of fear. Fear is a natural reaction that helps keep us safe. Bravery is doing what we know needs to be done, in spite of our fear.

We usually think of Bravery as racing through a hail of bullets to rescue a fallen comrade or carrying someone from a burning building. But people fear failing in business or a relationship, losing a race, or being turned down for a date.

Scouts learn to be Brave every day by standing up for the ideas, people, and institutions they believe in and by telling the truth in all situations. They conquer fears such as rejection and public speaking through fundraising and by earning Merit Badges.

While we won't see this type of Bravery in action movies, these fears are real, many of us have them, and overcoming them requires Bravery. Our lives are constantly changing, and it appears easier and safer to just stay in our ruts. Making a change requires Bravery.

It would be hard to think of anyone more qualified to speak of Bravery than former Chairman of the Joint Chiefs of Staff, General Henry H. Shelton. His comments about Scouting and Bravery are inspirational.

SCOUTING BUILDS
GREAT AMERICANS

A s a Scout, or perhaps a potential Scout, you are no doubt anxious to grow up, to take your place in society, and to become a man. I felt the same way at your age but, over the years, I have learned that manhood is not really about age, or about having a job, driving a car, or owning a place to live.

Manhood is knowing the difference between right and wrong and having the moral courage to choose the honorable course of action. It means taking responsibility for your actions, always telling the truth, regardless of the consequences, and helping those less fortunate.

It is also looking beyond yourself so that you can make a positive contribution to your family, troop, community, and country. Manhood is really living your life by the right values, which is the cornerstone of Scouting.

There are countless examples of remarkable acts accomplished by young people because they were influenced and motivated by the values promoted in Scouting. From saving lives to performing community service, young men like you make a difference in the places where you live.

I am especially proud of another group of young Americans who also live by the same values that you learn through Scouting. These remarkable young people, including many former Boy Scouts, wear the uniform of our Armed Forces and serve in every part of the world—on land, at sea, and in the air—protecting the Nation and our way of life.

They are keeping the peace in Bosnia and Kosovo, a troubled land that has witnessed tremendous suffering. In the Persian Gulf, American soldiers, sailors, airmen, marines, and coastguardsmen remain in place to ensure the security of our friends and allies in that vital region. And on the Korean peninsula, 37,000 American servicemen and women, along with our South Korean allies, are standing guard against the million-man North Korean Peoples Army. Just as the Boy Scouts show young men at their very best, our young men and women in uniform show our country at its very best. They serve all over the world, not only safeguarding America's interests, but also upholding and promoting America's values. These are many of the same values learned in Scouting.

A few years ago, an experience confirmed my unshakable faith in the young people of America. During Operation DESERT STORM, I served with the 101st Airborne Division, the "Screaming Eagles." On February 25, 1991, the evening before we were to launch the ground war against Iraqi forces in Kuwait and southern Iraq, I stood on a knoll and looked down on 325 helicopters that were dispersed across the Saudi desert.

Illuminated by the twilight, I could see a number of American pilots and infantrymen next to each helicopter, and I suddenly realized that many of these young soldiers were still in their teens.

I could see them standing quietly, or calmly sitting in small groups beside their helicopters, ready to launch just before dawn the next morning. You could sense their determination and courage.

When the time for liftoff arrived, they climbed into their helicopters, checked their weapons and ammunition, and became the "lightning in the Storm" as they successfully defeated Saddam's army.

The performance of these young troops in combat was simply tremendous that day, and every succeeding day during the Gulf War. Most impressive was their strength of character, their poise, and their courage. The night before the battle, they weren't concerned about themselves. They talked about the importance of the mission and worried about their buddies.

None of them asked, "What's in this for me?" None of them asked, "Can't we take the easy way out?" or "Why are we doing this?" Instead, they did their jobs to the best of their abilities. They served selflessly and this is one of the key lessons of Scouting.

Like the young soldiers in the deserts of Kuwait and Iraq, Boy Scouts today demonstrate selfless service whenever they volunteer for community service projects, take care of other people in need, and help to make our country a better place to live.

As you continue your life's journey to manhood, my advice to each of you is to live every day by the values of Scouting. People will recognize and appreciate those special qualities, and you will be successful in life.

Best wishes to you and your fellow Scouts on that journey.

GENERAL HENRY H. SHELTON
Former Chairman of the Joint Chiefs of Staff

General Henry Shelton began his military career through the ROTC program at North Carolina State University. He served two tours of duty in Vietnam, a tour in Saudi Arabia for Operation Desert Storm, and numerous stateside commands. General Shelton has been awarded the Defense Distinguished Service Medal, Distinguished Service Medal, Legion of Merit, Bronze Star, and Purple Heart.

As the fourteenth Chairman of the Joint Chiefs of Staff, he served as the principal military advisor to the President, the Secretary of Defense, and the National Security Council. For more details about General Shelton's life and career, visit http://www.npr.org/programs/npc/001214.hshelton.html.

General Shelton's letter was written before September 11, 2001, which is why he did not mention our brave troops currently battling terrorism.

BRAVERY

Below are some actions you can take to be Brave today and space to address some of your own personal fears. Check them off as you deal with them.

❑ Refuse to succumb to peer pressure to indulge in smoking, sex, alcohol, or drugs.

❑ Stand by a friend who is being picked on.

❑ Ask someone out who you have wanted to ask but have been afraid of possible rejection.

❑ Don't let embarrassment about being overweight keep you from joining a gym to get in shape.

❑ Get on with your life after a scare, don't let yourself become paralyzed by fear.

❑ If you would like to be an entrepreneur, research a business and assess the risks and rewards.

❑ Take a class in self-defense.

❑ Wear clothes you enjoy, don't be afraid to go against the current fad.

❑ Push beyond your comfort zone. Take on a difficult project at work or an advanced class at school.

❑ When you get thrown off your horse (figuratively or literally), dust yourself off and get right back on.

❑ Reject pressure to join a gang.

❑ Work on overcoming a fear. If it's public speaking, join Toastmasters. If you are afraid of flying, heights, or crowds, try counseling, meditation, or hypnosis.

❑ Learn to ride a bike or swim.

❑ Refuse to be intimidated by technology. Take a class or buy a book and learn how to master it.

❑ Get a check-up by your doctor or dentist. You may be afraid of them but they protect you from far greater dangers.

❑ Try a new food.

❑ Push yourself past your comfort point, physically, by walking or riding your bike further than usual. But, be careful not to injure yourself.

❑ Let your children grow up. As parents, we are afraid to let them get hurt—physically or emotionally. However, in order to reach their potential as independent people they must learn to think, make judgments, act, and take responsibility for themselves.

❑ _____

❑ _____

❑ _____

❑ _____

❑ _____

The harder the conflict, the more glorious the triumph. What we obtain too cheap, we esteem too lightly; it is dearness only that gives everything its value.

I love the man that can smile in trouble, that can gather strength from distress and grow brave by reflection. 'Tis the business of little minds to shrink; but he whose heart is firm, and whose conscience approves his conduct, will pursue his principles unto death.

THOMAS PAINE

DAY 12

THRIFTY

Using resources wisely, careful in spending, economical.

Thrifty is saving money but also much more. It is using everything wisely not wastefully, and getting the most value out of it.

Scouts know that being Thrifty means buying the best value, not just the cheapest price. Cheap is not necessarily Thrifty, particularly with items such as hiking boots and climbing gear.

This applies outside Scouting, too, in critical areas such as file servers, employees, and brakes for our car. Being overly Thrifty (or cheap) can actually cost us far more in the long run than we saved initially.

In addition to conserving money, Thrifty means managing other assets such as time, energy, and natural resources, wisely. We should work smarter, not harder. Rather than driving to the hardware store numerous times for additional items, we can plan out our project, reduce the number of trips, and save gas and time.

We can ensure that we get the best value by making informed buying decisions utilizing Consumer Reports, www.Cnet.com, www.ZDnet.com, and other product evaluation publications and websites before we buy.

Thrifty Scouts and Scouters consider *cost of ownership* not just initial purchase price. For products that use consumables, such as copiers and printers, we usually spend more on supplies, over the life of the product, than we paid for the item itself.

In today's *Scouting Way* story, consumer advocate David Horowitz, a man who has made a career of Thriftiness, shares his code about getting a fair deal.

FIGHT BACK!

I have always thought of Scouting as a great tool to instill values in young boys and girls. I have a statement that I have lived by for many years:

*Life is full of compromise, but to compromise
principle is to give up your self-respect.
I don't want anyone to take me for a sucker,
and I don't like to see anyone else taken, either.*

*A lot of things are unfair in life. It's tough;
that's the way it is. But, by heaven,
if you can do something about it, do it.*

DAVID HOROWITZ
Consumer Advocate
Host of *Fight Back! with David Horowitz*

David Horowitz is well known for his Emmy-winning *Fight Back! with David Horowitz* television series, syndicated newspaper columns, books, and radio features. He has spent his career researching the facts and educating consumers.

He also guides young people toward careers as consumer affairs professionals through his non-profit Fight Back! Foundation. For more information about David Horowitz, visit www.FightBack.com

THRIFTINESS

Here are some suggestions for being Thrifty. Add your own in the blanks and put a checkmark next to each one you do.

❑ Plant drought-tolerant plants in your yard.

❑ Rather than finance a major purchase, such as a car, consider getting a home equity loan and paying cash. Finance charges are no longer tax deductible but home loan interest may be.

❑ Turn off extra lights and appliances to save energy.

❑ Instead of buying an extravagant item, put the money into savings.

❑ Buy recycled paper products.

❑ Consider buying a new refrigerator. A new energy efficient one may save energy and money in the long run.

❑ Buy large economy packs of meats and breads, then repackage and freeze them at home.

❑ Use a solar blanket to heat your pool.

❑ Spend the extra money to buy a quality tent, pair of hiking boots, climbing harness, or other item you will use and depend upon for years.

❑ Put on a sweater instead of turning up the thermostat.

❑ Have a garage sale—recycle your treasures and earn money, too.

❑ Replace your furnace filter.

❑ Add weather stripping to keep the cold out and reduce your heating bills.

❑ Save water and money by fixing a dripping faucet.

❑ Tune up your car to improve gas mileage and reduce emissions.

❑ Clip coupons, either from a newspaper or online at sites such as www.CoolSavings.com or www.CouponSurfer.com.

❑ Start a rainy-day fund.

❑ Get a quote on refinancing your house at a lower rate. Be sure to factor the loan costs into your decision.

❑ Put lights on timers.

❑ Meet with your accountant at least once a year to plan your tax strategy.

❑ Install solar panels on your home.

❑ Organize your errands to make the most efficient use of your time and gasoline.

❑ Ride your bicycle or walk short distances instead of driving your car.

❑ _____

❑ _____

❑ _____

❑ _____

❑ _____

Beware of little expenses.
A small leak will sink a great ship.

BENJAMIN FRANKLIN

DAY 13

DO A GOOD TURN DAILY

Doing something for someone without being asked to, or expecting payment for it, each day.

D oing a Good Turn Daily is synonymous with Scouting. Rather than a specific value, such as Trustworthy, Scouting's slogan is a mindset which encompasses many Scouting values including being Kind, Courteous, Helpful, and Friendly.

Everywhere we look there is an opportunity to help someone. Some Good Deeds are big, others small. The important thing is to get in the habit of looking for them—and doing them.

Since service projects are such a core element of Scouting, we can think of Doing a Good Turn Daily as a lifelong service project.

Doing a Good Turn is something to look forward to every day because each Good Deed can be different. It is a way of sharing a smile from our heart. Every Good Turn Makes the World a Better Place.

As Speaker of the House Dennis Hastert demonstrates in today's *Scouting Way* anecdote, a seemingly insignificant Good Turn can have a global impact.

BECAUSE OF ONE SCOUT'S GOOD DEED

The values of one boy changed America. And he happened to be from England.

An American traveler—from my home state of Illinois—found himself a bit lost one night on the foggy streets of London, England. This American was in quite a hurry to a business meeting, but simply couldn't navigate through the thick London fog.

Just when he thought it was a lost cause, a young Englishman approached and asked, "May I be of service to you?"

The American replied, "Yes," and explain where he needed to go.

The English boy said, "Follow me, Sir," and happily led him to his destination.

Being a typical American, the man from Ottawa, Illinois offered the boy a shilling for his help. The lad refused, saying: "I do not accept tips for courtesies." The boy told him that his mentor had taught him to do a good turn daily. The American was impressed.

While we never learned who the young boy was that fateful foggy night, we do know that the American traveler was William D. Boyce, who after a business meeting on that same night in 1908, asked the young boy to lead him to his mentor. His mentor was Robert Baden-Powell, the founder of Scouting in Great Britain.

Two years later, Boyce and others founded the Boy Scouts of America. Since then, more than 100 million young men have had the Scouting experience—and uncountable others have been helped by their good works.

What always amazes me is that all of this happened because of a young Scout from England who did a good deed. That truly attests to how far good values can take us.

Now, more than ever, we can appreciate a group that teaches young men about the importance of personal responsibility and moral values. The Boy Scouts—to put it simply—are a training ground for good Americans. I know firsthand; years ago, I had the honor of serving as an Explorer troop leader.

The Boy Scouts help young men develop values that they will carry with them throughout their lives. The Scouting experience extends beyond being prepared, doing a good turn daily, taking the Boy Scout Oath and adhering to the Boy Scout Law.

The young men who start out in the Boy Scouts grow up to be good citizens and to respect America. They live their lives defending its honor and standing up for its principles, both in words and in deeds.

If every American citizen went through this kind of program, I can only imagine the country we would live in. Fittingly, Congress recognized the Boy Scouts' contribution to our nation early on. The Boy Scouts helped the World War I effort by selling bonds and collecting paper and metal for recycling.

So, in 1916—just six years after the Boy Scouts were founded in America—Congress thanked them by granting them a special Congressional charter.

As a Congressman, and as an American, I'm proud to be part of a body that supports the Boy Scouts. They are truly a national treasure.

J. DENNIS HASTERT
Congressman from Illinois
Speaker of the House

J. Dennis Hastert was born in Aurora, Illinois and graduated from Wheaton College and Northern Illinois University. After teaching high school for 16 years, he spent 6 years in the Illinois House of Representatives before being elected to the U.S. House of Representatives. For more information about Speaker Dennis Hastert, see www.house.gov/hastert/.

As a freelance magazine cartoonist, before becoming syndicated, the name of the game was PERSEVERENCE. Without it, very few reach success.

When I launched my cartoon panel that appealed to family members of all ages, the material had to be CLEAN and REVERENT.

Amidst questionable entertainment on all sides, every day for more than four decades *Family Circus* has touched millions of lives.

Somewhere along the way HUMBLENESS may have gotten lost, but I'm proud and confident that I'm doing a GOOD TURN DAILY.

BIL KEANE
Creator of *The Family Circus*

GOOD TURNS

*Below are some Good Turns plus space to include your own.
Do a Good Turn Daily, starting today, and check it off.*

❑ Take your neighbor's empty trashcans up to their gate.

❑ Offer to pick something up at the store for an elderly
or sick neighbor.

❑ When a driver signals to change into your lane, back
off and let them in.

❑ Prepare dinner for your spouse and let them sit and relax.

❑ Notify a manager about a child wandering around a
store, looking lost and scared.

❑ Try to find the owner of a parked car with its lights left on.

❑ Offer to give a neighbor's child a ride home from
school on a rainy day.

❑ Pick up litter and throw it away.

❑ Use your knowledge of the outdoors or another subject
to help someone less knowledgeable in that area.

❑ Put out a smoldering fire you find while hiking.

❑ Help someone having trouble putting gas in their car
or air in their tires.

❑ Bring extra food on a campout or picnic and share it.

❑ Feed an expired parking meter (unless it's illegal where
you are).

❑ Stop for a pedestrian trying to cross the street at a corner.

❑ Let a shopper buying only a few items go ahead of you
in line.

❑ Take lecture notes for a classmate who is absent.

❑ Call 911 or another emergency number to report an accident or a stranded motorist.

❑ Help someone get a heavy item into their shopping cart or car.

❑ On a rainy morning, when you go outside to get your newspaper, put your neighbor's newspaper on their doorstep.

❑ When a driver signals to change into your lane, back off and let them in.

❑ Hold the door open for someone.

❑ At a school or Scout event, take pictures of a child whose parents are not present or who do not have a camera.

❑ Pull out an extra shopping cart for another shopper.

❑ Fix a computer or other item for someone who cannot afford to buy a new one.

❑ _____

❑ _____

❑ _____

❑ _____

❑ _____

How far that little candle throws its beams! So shines a good deed in a naughty world.

WILLIAM SHAKESPEARE

DAY 14

LET SOMEONE ELSE SHINE

*Allowing another person to have credit for
something positive. Modest, humble, not self-centered.*

We all want to be recognized for our ideas and hard work. But you will be amazed how good it feels to Let Someone Else Shine, particularly young people.

Scout leaders know the feeling—as do teachers and youth sports coaches—seeing kids standing straighter, smiling proudly, at their success.

Scouts are Humble, never boastful. They shine through their deeds rather than their words and are quick to share credit. Letting Someone Else Shine, at any age, helps their self-esteem and inspires them to attempt new feats.

As Harriet Woods said, "You can stand tall without standing on someone. You can be a victor without having victims." Scouts and leaders know how wonderful it is to stand near someone in the spotlight. Life isn't always about us.

In today's *Scouting Way* story Ken Venturi, a great golfer and true gentleman, gives a clinic in graciousness and Letting Someone Else Shine.

STAYING THE COURSE

A ll of the values Scouting tries to instill in their young men I hopefully have tried to respect in my lifetime. One story that you might enjoy would emphasize the rule "Let someone else shine."

Back in 1953 when Byron Nelson took me under his wing, we played a lot of golf at several golf courses. I noticed that before we played he always inquired of someone at the golf course, "What is the course record and who holds it?"

I finally asked him why he always asked that question before we played and he said to me: "Ken, you always find out what the course record is, and if it is held by the home pro, you never break it, for he lives there and we are only visiting."

In other words, "Let someone else shine."

Of course, if a tournament is played there, that is a different situation, but I never forgot what he said. He knew what it meant to let someone else shine.

KEN VENTURI
Golfer and Broadcaster

Ken Venturi's storied career includes winning the U.S. Open, selection to the Ryder Cup Team, being named *PGA Player of the Year*, and *Sports Illustrated's Sportsman of the Year*.

When illness forced him into retirement as a player he overcame severe stuttering to become the nation's top golf commentator, according to *Golf Digest*. For details about Ken Venturi, see www.golfweb.com/u/ce/multi/pgatour/0,1977,2181419,00.html.

LET SOMEONE ELSE SHINE

Here are some thoughts for Letting Someone Else Shine. Be sure to add your own as well. Check them off as you carry them out.

❑ Acknowledge someone else's hard work: How nice your spouse (or parent) keeps the house, how diligently your children study to get good grades, how hard your spouse (or parent) works to provide for your family.

❑ When someone tells a story, resist the impulse to top them with a tale of your own.

❑ Think of something to congratulate your kids about in everything they attempt.

❑ When you read about someone (or their parents or children) in the newspaper, cut it out and send it to them.

❑ Praise your kids, Scouts, or co-workers in front of their peers.

❑ Write a letter to a person's supervisor when they give you terrific service.

❑ Compliment the cook. If the food isn't to your liking, how about the presentation, dishes, or flowers?

❑ Praise a young parent doing a good job handling a tough situation with their child.

❑ Find something to compliment when you visit a person's home or office.

❑ Call or write someone to congratulate them on a promotion, graduation, or other achievement.

❑ Recommend a doctor, dentist, or other service provider who does great work.

❑ Give someone else top billing for a project well done.

❑ Publicly acknowledge the important role of your helper in a successful endeavor.

❑ Resist the urge to lecture children in front of their friends or classmates. Wait until you are alone, and calm.

❑ When correcting a person's work, particularly a child's, praise their efforts in another part of the project. If they perceive themselves as a failure in all areas they may not be motivated to improve. However, if some of their efforts are paying off, they will be more inclined to want to improve their weak areas.

❑ Ask your parents or grandparents what life was like before inventions such as televisions, VCR's, microwave ovens, and computers.

❑ _____

❑ _____

❑ _____

❑ _____

❑ _____

*An automobile goes nowhere efficiently unless it has
a quick, hot spark to ignite things, to set the cogs of
the machine in motion. So I try to make every
player on my team feel he's the spark keeping our
machine in motion. On him depends our success.*

KNUTE ROCKNE

DAY 15

KIND

Gentle-hearted, considerate of others, doing good rather than harm.

Kindness is like a smile. It's free, always appreciated, and can start a chain reaction that brightens the day far beyond the person to whom we gave it.

A Kind act toward a friend or loved one reminds them that we care and makes them feel valuable. This is vital in creating lasting relationships and will generate reciprocal acts of Kindness.

Kindness shown to a stranger, as in a Good Deed, can be magical because it is unexpected. It reminds them that in our sometimes impersonal world, people still care about other people—even those with whom they have no connection.

In addition to practicing Kindness itself, Scouting teaches us to incorporate Kindness into other values, such as Leadership. The same information can be conveyed harshly or softly. The Kindest, and most effective, way is the one that takes the feelings of others into account.

In today's *Scouting Way* tale, Famous Amos Founder Wally Amos shares a recipe for Kindness and shows how quickly its delicious aroma can spread to brighten the lives of others.

KINDNESS

L et's focus on how we can make other people happy.

Recently, while we were having dinner, my friend Tracey told me about shopping for a gift for her mother during Christmas in a store with extremely long lines. She found her gift and noticed there was no line at the cashier in that area.

She made her purchase, and then went to the end of the long line and discreetly told the last person in the line that there was no waiting in the other area and advised her to go there to pay for her purchase. However, she said, before you leave the store share the news with the last person in line and tell them to do the same.

Later that afternoon she was in an office meeting and a fellow worker shared the story that she was last in line after shopping and someone...you get the picture. Tracey said she felt so good that she yelled out, "I started that!" She received tremendous joy from performing an act of kindness.

On a more personal note, I was returning to Hawaii from a trip and the pilot admired my watermelon hat and said he was going to wrestle me for it. I told him he had no chance.

After we landed he came out of the cockpit and said he had come for my hat. I told him he couldn't have it. No way! He began stating his case, telling me what a great collection of hats he had. I still said no.

All of a sudden, a little voice said, "Give him the hat!" I asked him to meet me outside the door and took my prized watermelon hat off and presented it to him, with the promise that he would wear it and not hang it on his wall. He put it on immediately, beaming from ear to ear.

When I departed the next day, a friend said he saw the pilot leave earlier that day and he was wearing *his* watermelon hat as the plane backed out of the gate.

Kindness is contagious; pass it on.

WALLY AMOS
Founder, Famous Amos

Wally "Famous" Amos went from high-school dropout to founder of a $10 million company to losing the rights to his own name to inspirational TV host and author. But, through it all, he has retained his infectious enthusiasm and love of people.

For details about Wally Amos and his *Wallymelon Credo* go to www.wallyamos.com.

Showing Kindness

The following are a few suggestions for showing Kindness and blank space for you to add others. Check off each way you show Kindness today.

❑ Play peek-a-boo with a fussy baby in line at a store.

❑ Think of a Kind thing to say to someone who is feeling a little down.

❑ Make a favorite bread or dessert. Prepare extra and share it with a neighbor or friend.

❑ Return your grocery cart to the rack.

❑ Tuck a little note inside your child or spouse's lunch. It will brighten their day.

❑ Give your pet a new toy, such as an old tennis ball for a dog or a ball of yarn for a cat.

❑ Offer criticism so constructively that the recipient is energized to go back and improve their work.

❑ Leave the postal carrier a cold drink on a hot day or a warm one on a cold day.

❑ Give someone a flower.

❑ Put out breadcrumbs for the wild birds after a winter snowstorm.

❑ Call or e-mail a friend or relative you haven't spoken to recently.

❑ Stay home from school or work when you are sick so that you do not infect others.

❏ Take a hot cup of cocoa to a crossing guard on a blustery day.

❏ When you park in a driveway, leave the sidewalk clear so that people can easily walk past.

❏ Refill the printer or copy machine after you have used a lot of paper.

❏ Bring in a tasty holiday treat and share it with your co-workers.

❏ Send someone a newspaper clipping or address for a website you think they would enjoy.

❏ Bring a meal to the family of a friend or neighbor who is under the weather.

❏ Take your dog to a dog park to let them run free and play with other dogs. Or, if have another type of pet, play with them.

❏ Pick your kids up from school on a rainy day when they would normally walk home.

❏ _____

❏ _____

❏ _____

❏ _____

❏ _____

*Kindness is the language which the deaf can hear
and the blind can see.*

MARK TWAIN

DAY 16

MAKE THE WORLD
A BETTER PLACE

Improving the world around us.
Leaving a positive legacy.

We would all like to think that we have a positive influence on the world around us. The trick is fitting that aspiration in with our other desires and obligations.

For most of us, with families depending on us and careers in progress, going off to India to carry on Mother Theresa's work simply is not a viable option.

Fortunately, Scouting teaches us that just by Doing a Good Turn Daily (like being Friendly, Honest, Kind, or Helpful) we are Making the World a Better Place.

Many of the ways Scouts Make the World a Better Place, such as food and clothing drives, can be organized by companies, neighborhoods, and other non-Scout organizations, too.

We must also focus on the legacy we are building, every day, with our children. The lessons they learn from us—intentional and inadvertent, positive and negative—will ripple through future generations.

Thanks to leaders like former McDonnell Douglas Chairman Sanford McDonnell companies, as well, can Make the World a Better Place.

THE SCOUTING WAY AT McDONNELL DOUGLAS

In 1983, after years of encouraging young people to live up to the values of the Scout Oath and Law, I asked myself how well was I doing against that wonderful code of ethics and found that I had a lot of room for improvement.

Then I asked myself about our employees. Surely they knew we wanted them to be ethical, but by what values? All corporations have a code of conduct which, in essence, is a 'thou shalt not' code. Not enough corporations have a positive 'thou shalt' code of ethics.

I formed a task force of vice presidents who reported directly to me, gave them the Scout Oath and Law, and asked them to design a code of ethics for McDonnell Douglas around the Oath and Law.

After a number of iterations, they came up with a great code of ethics that covered every point except 'A Scout is reverent.' As a Christian, I would like to think that all of our employees believe in God, but I had to concede that we could not use my executive position in the corporation to pressure them to be reverent.

We adopted that code of ethics unanimously at our April 1983 Board of Directors meeting, and we didn't just hang it on the wall.

We set up training programs to teach all of us including me, the chairman and chief executive officer, how to use it in our daily business lives. It was an eight-hour experience that was mandatory for all personnel. By the time I retired in 1988, we had trained over 50,000 people.

Since 1988 I have spent my retirement career getting character education into the schools K-12, with the goal of making the values of Scouting a part of every young person's character. The Boy Scouts of America has been a profound and major influence in my life.

SANFORD MCDONNELL
Chairman Emeritus, McDonnell Douglas

During World War II, Sanford McDonnell, nephew of McDonnell Aircraft founder James S. McDonnell, worked on the Manhattan Project, which developed the atomic bomb. At McDonnell Aircraft, Mr. McDonnell developed combat aircraft before being elected President of the company.

He is a former national President of the Boy Scouts of America and was honored as St. Louis Man of the Year.

For further information about Sanford McDonnell, visit www.boeing.com/companyoffices/history/mdc/snm.htm.

MAKE THE WORLD A BETTER PLACE

Here are some things you can do today to Make the World a Better Place and blank space for you to add your own. Check them off as you do them.

❑ Pick up litter and throw it away (and, of course, never litter yourself).

❑ Plant flowers or a tree.

❑ Organize a community service event for your Scout unit, school, or company.

❑ Donate time or money to a worthwhile cause or charity.

❑ If your car is spewing pollution, get it fixed even if you have not gotten a ticket yet.

❑ Smile.

❑ Be a low-impact camper. Always leave your campsite as pristine as you found it (or better). And, observe fire restrictions.

❑ Start a Scout unit in a new area.

❑ Create a group to find a solution for a problem in your community.

❑ Work for a candidate who is truly committed to improving the system.

❑ Become a Big Brother or Big Sister.

❑ Clean out your garage or closet and donate items you no longer use to a local charity or thrift store.

❑ Use rechargeable batteries.

❑ When you change the oil in your car, take the old oil to a recycling center, don't just dump it. Recycle old mercury thermometers, too.

❑ If you have moved to a new area and your old town had a great way to solve a common problem, share it with your new community.

❑ Show tolerance toward someone of another race, religion, or nationality.

❑ Organize a group to clean up an eyesore in your town.

❑ Start a community garden. Plant an extra row and give the produce to your local food bank.

❑ Attend a school board or city council meeting.

❑ Donate free clicks on the Internet. You can raise money for causes such as world hunger, saving the rainforests, and cancer research just by clicking on sites like www.TheHungerSite.com and www.Good-Deed.dhs.org.

❑ _____

❑ _____

❑ _____

❑ _____

❑ _____

To laugh often and much; to win the respect of intelligent people and the affection of children...to leave the world a better place...to know even one life has breathed easier because you have lived. This is to have succeeded.

RALPH WALDO EMERSON

DAY 17

TRUSTWORTHY

True to your word, honoring your commitments.
Can be depended upon.

The first Boy Scout Law, Trustworthy, is at the very foundation of any relationship. If our spouse, children, friends, or co-workers can't trust us (and vice versa) what kind of relationship can we have? They must believe that our word is gold.

Scouts know that our Honor lives in our word. When we say something, it is true (to the best of our knowledge). When we make a promise, we keep it. We are people who can be trusted.

Money and possessions may come and go but our credibility, our code as a person, is ours forever—good or bad. Trustworthiness is the keystone of our integrity. No one can take it away from us, but we can destroy it—or rebuild it.

Trustworthiness is particularly important in our elected representatives so we hope they all hear former Senator and astronaut Jake Garn's message loud and clear.

TRUSTWORTHY

I believe that being trustworthy is one of the most important values that anyone can have. Always being openly and directly honest served me exceptionally well during twenty-five years of public service.

Sometimes the truth is painful in the short run but, in the long run, the rewards are overwhelming.

One should understand that, if you always tell the truth, you don't have to remember what you said yesterday, last week or last year.

E.J. "JAKE" GARN
Retired Senator from Utah
Space Shuttle Discovery Astronaut

Senator E.J. "Jake" Garn is a true aviator at heart. He was a private pilot and a pilot in both the Navy and Air Guard. Ten years after becoming a U.S. Senator from Utah, Senator Garn spent almost a week in space as a Payload Specialist aboard the Space Shuttle Discovery.

For more information about Senator Jake Garn, check out http://vesuvius.jsc.nasa.gov/er/seh/garn.htm.

TRUSTWORTHY

The following are ways to be Trustworthy. As always, add your own, too. Look for opportunities, today, to put Trustworthiness to work and check them off.

❑ Make a commitment and follow through with it. It can be as small as reading a story to a child, taking out the trash, or making a favorite dessert. As parents, our children need to see us live up to our obligations. Otherwise, they will make the same mistake.

❑ If someone tells you a juicy secret that you just can't wait to talk about, honor the confidence (unless it will harm someone).

❑ Don't park in a spot reserved for the handicapped (unless you are handicapped). As you walk the extra distance, be thankful that you can.

❑ Return something you borrowed without waiting to be asked. Always return things in as good or better condition than you received them.

❑ Make sure your computer has current virus protection software. Some viruses automatically send themselves out to all your e-mail addresses. People must be able to trust that the e-mail they receive from you is safe.

❑ Refrain from sampling the food as you go through the grocery store.

❑ When a driver is driving safely by leaving space between them and the car ahead, they are trusting other drivers not to use that space to cut in and make it unsafe. Honor that trust.

❑ Admit a mistake promptly and fix the damage, without being asked.

❑ Buy software or music rather than bootlegging a copy.

❑ When you receive an e-mail asking you to forward it to everyone you know, first verify that it's not a hoax at sites like www.UrbanLegends.about.com or www.Symantec.com/avcenter/hoax.html.

❑ Return library books and rented videos on time.

❑ If you tell a salesperson that you are looking to buy a product and they give you good information, buy it from them. Don't have them spend their valuable time with you then purchase the item on the web or at another store, just to save money.

❑ _____

❑ _____

❑ _____

❑ _____

❑ _____

Tom does everything well. He's the kind of man you'd want your kids to grow up to be like. Tom's a studious player, devoted to his profession, a loyal cat, trustworthy—everything a Boy Scout's supposed to be. In fact, we call him "Boy Scout."

CLEON JONES
regarding Hall of Fame pitcher Tom Seaver

DAY 18

CONTINUE TO LEARN

*An unceasing quest for knowledge. Developing new
skills and seeking new ideas throughout your life.*

C ontinuing to Learn is a fundamental tenet of Scouting.
The more we learn, the richer our lives become. When
we are continually engaged in creative thought and expand-
ing our horizons, we are more interesting—and so is life.

We have all said, "Someday I want to learn how to…"
Whether it's woodworking, quilting, playing a musical
instrument, sailing, or using a computer, now is the time. As
the old saying goes, "Use it or lose it."

There are courses available at community centers and
colleges everywhere. We can check out a how-to book from
the library or take classes at home on the Internet. There is
probably a web site or chat room about anything we could
want to learn.

Beyond the obvious benefits, keeping our mind active
reduces the likelihood of developing ailments such as
Alzheimer's Disease.

We can learn a lot from the mistakes of others. So let's
listen carefully to what self-made millionaire and Wendy's
founder, Dave Thomas, considers his biggest mistake in
today's *Scouting Way* anecdote.

My Biggest Mistake

When I was 15, I made the biggest mistake of my life by dropping out of high school. I stayed behind while my family moved out of state, so I was living at the YMCA in Fort Wayne, Indiana, going to school and working full-time.

I knew I wanted to have a career in the restaurant business, so I figured I could learn more by working than in school. So I quit school and made the biggest mistake of my life.

It bothered me for many years, but I managed to forget about it most of the time. Being a "drop-out" is not something to be proud of. Despite all the success I'd had in the restaurant industry, all the awards I'd received and the honorary degrees I had from Duke and Clemson Universities, I still didn't have a high school diploma.

In 1992, I was meeting with some high school students, telling them to stay in school and get all the education they could. One student asked me, "You're telling us to stay in school, yet you dropped out. How can you expect us to take advice that you didn't follow?"

That statement really made me think. He was right. Why didn't I go back and finish high school? I talked to my wife and children about it and they all encouraged me to go for it. So I did. I got a tutor and started studying for the GED exam. It wasn't easy. I was busy with Wendy's, traveling and making commercials and I still had to find time to study.

But in 1993, 45 years after leaving high school, I received my GED certificate and high school diploma. It remains one of my greatest accomplishments. I was so proud to be able to say I'd finished high school, and proved that it's never too late to finish what you start and get your GED.

By the way, I was made an honorary member of the 1993 senior class at Coconut Creek High School, near my home in Ft. Lauderdale, Florida. They named me "Most Likely to Succeed." And my wife Lorraine and I even got to go to the prom where we were crowned Prom King and Queen!

DAVE THOMAS
Founder of Wendy's

Dave Thomas began working in the restaurant business at age 12 and became a millionaire at 35. Later, he founded Wendy's, named after his eight year-old daughter.

As an adopted kid who never knew his birth parents, Mr. Thomas is an adoption advocate and founded the Dave Thomas Foundation for Adoption.

For more information about Dave Thomas, visit http://www.wendys.com/dave_history/meet_dave.html.

CONTINUING TO LEARN

Below are a few suggestions for Continuing to Learn and blank space to add your own. Be sure to check them off, each month, as you practice them.

❑ Always have two books you are reading: one fun and one learning.

❑ Read a daily newspaper or a weekly news magazine.

❑ Talk to your kids, you will be amazed at how much they know.

❑ Learn to play a musical instrument.

❑ Take a class at your local community center or college and make a new friend.

❑ Learn a new language.

❑ Read the Science & Technology sections of newspapers and magazines.

❑ Travel.

❑ If you are a retired executive, join SCORE (Service Corps. Of Retired Executives). Although, officially, you are teaching others you will be surprised how much you learn yourself.

❑ Learn about new ideas and technology such as computers or the Internet.

❑ Instead of listening to the radio while driving, learn a new language or skill by listening to instructional tapes or CD's.

❑ Try out a fun, new recipe.

❑ Learn to play a new sport.

❏ Go to the library and browse the shelves for new areas to explore.

❏ Watch the Discovery or History Channels.

❏ Go to a museum. Beside paintings and dinosaurs, there are museums dedicated to aviation, dolls, trains, and almost anything else you could imagine.

❏ Have lunch or dinner in a type of restaurant you have never tried before.

❏ Visit a science or technology fair.

❏ Learn a new computer application, either by taking a class or reading a book.

❏ Take up a new hobby.

❏ Get your GED or go back to college. Start a new degree program or finish an old one.

❏ Ask someone with a job that interests you how they got where they are today.

❏ _____

❏ _____

❏ _____

❏ _____

❏ _____

Anyone who stops learning is old, whether at twenty or eighty. Anyone who keeps learning stays young. The greatest thing in life is to keep your mind young.

HENRY FORD

DAY 19

RESPONSIBLE FOR WHAT I SAY AND DO

Thinking through your actions beforehand and accepting responsibility for the results. Not passing the buck or playing the Blame Game. Taking an active role in determining an outcome.

A lmost daily we hear about someone acting thoughtlessly and then blaming others. They drive with hot coffee in their lap, spill it, then sue the restaurant for their burns. Or kill someone and claim Hostess Twinkies were responsible.

Scouting develops responsibility. We learn that we have an obligation to ourselves and others to consider the consequences of our actions before we take them, and accept responsibility for those actions afterwards. Therefore, we must think rather than act impulsively.

Responsibility is frequently equated with accountability, as in acknowledging responsibility for a result. However, Scouting's emphasis on Leadership also trains us to be responsible by actively affecting the outcome.

So, while Scouts do accept responsibility, after the fact, for the success or failure of their team, they don't just sit idly by waiting for the outcome. They jump into the fray, while the game is on, working hard to advance their cause.

It is much easier to accept responsibility for a result when we have also been responsible for crafting it.

We have choices in life, however we must look hard to see all our options. Success comes from choosing wisely, putting our whole being behind our choice, and accepting responsibility for the outcome, no matter what.

However, the *wise* choice is not always clear. Fortunately, Lou Holtz, a man who has made lots of tough choices as one of the most successful coaches in collegiate history, offers us his litmus test as a guide.

ON MY SHOULDER

L ife is full of choices, choices that can be difficult to make depending on the surroundings, circumstances or people in the area.

One of the guidelines that I have always used when it came time to decide between doing something wrong or right is this:

Imagine your mother on one side of you and God on the other. If you would still do it with both of them there, then it is probably the right thing to do.

This has always worked for my children and me. It is hard to believe that these two individuals would lead us astray.

LOU HOLTZ
Head Football Coach, University of South Carolina
Former Head Football Coach, Notre Dame

Coach Lou Holtz won 100 games in 11 seasons at Notre Dame. In his 27 years as a collegiate head coach, he is third on the all-time list of winning active Division I-A coaches.

Coach Holtz drives his players to excellence both on the field and off. He is the only coach to win a national championship and achieve a 100% graduation rate in the same year. Unsurprisingly, he won *Coach of the Year* honors that year.

For more information about Coach Lou Holtz, see www.coachholtz.com/BiographyCareer/Biography.cfm.

RESPONSIBLE FOR
WHAT I SAY AND DO

Here are some ways to be Responsible for What You Say and Do. Add your own in the blanks. Check each one off as you accomplish it.

❑ Help your kids create a list of their responsibilities. Praise them for meeting their obligations.

❑ Start a notebook for a project to ensure that all the information is readily accessible and the project is easy to organize and track.

❑ Use a calendar such as Outlook (on your computer) or SuperCalendar (www.SuperCalendar.com on the Internet) to remind you of your commitments.

❑ Before criticizing, pause to consider how to phrase your criticism most constructively.

❑ Start or update your To Do list. Review it daily and move incomplete tasks to the top.

❑ Ask yourself if you are doing everything possible to achieve your desired outcome. If not, redouble your efforts.

❑ Do what you *have to do* before you do what you *want to do*—and ensure that you meet your obligations.

❑ Accept responsibility for your mistake, even if you have an opportunity to shift the blame. Be an example of how to handle an error graciously.

❑ Hold your temper even when you have been provoked.

❑ Calmly explain to a child or subordinate what they did wrong rather than yelling at them.

❑ Do your chores without being asked.

❑ Turn in your homework or report on time.

❑ Don't blame the weather or traffic for making you late, leave earlier next time.

❑ Get help if you are having problems with alcohol or drugs.

❑ Maintain a notebook or spreadsheet of your family's medical history.

❑ Get a ride home if you have had too much to drink or are too tired to drive safely.

❑ Take care of your pets. Make sure they have food, clean water, and dry shelter.

❑ _____

❑ _____

❑ _____

❑ _____

❑ _____

We must reject the idea that every time a law's broken, society is guilty rather than the lawbreaker. It is time to restore the American precept that each individual is accountable for his actions.

PRESIDENT RONALD REAGAN

DAY 20

COURTEOUS

Treating people with respect and consideration.
Being polite and well mannered.

Courtesy is the grease that reduces friction and helps human interaction run smoothly. At its core, being Courteous is simply knowing good behavior and manners and caring enough to use them.

Manners do not cost anything and are not difficult to use. It is a matter of being polite, not interrupting, not cutting people off in traffic, and listening to them.

Scouts know that "Please" and "Thank you" are words that make us feel good when we say them and are always nice to hear. They are the first words of Courtesy, but not the last.

Scouts and leaders consider the feelings of others. They know that how they deliver criticism can be as important as the comments themselves, so they always try to be constructive.

Courtesy, and the feelings it creates, generate ripples, which not only return Courtesy to us but spread its warmth to others as well. Scouter Pete Murray is our Merit Badge Counselor for Courtesy, in this *Scouting Way* saga.

THE CAMPOUT POLICE

I want to confess something to the group tonight. This past week I was stopped by a cop. Yeah, it happened on the new road 414, too. I came over the hill and there they were; there were four of them. At first sight, my heart leapt into my throat, the hair on the back of my neck stood up, and I began to sweat.

I looked at the speedometer and saw that I was doing a mile or two under the speed limit, and still I was panicky. The first thought to hit me was that saying... "The guilty flee when no one pursues," and then it happened. The policeman stepped out into the road and waved for me to stop.

Now my mind was really racing...what DID I do? Was just driving on this road going to get me a ticket? Well, by the time these and a thousand other thoughts raced through my head I had pulled over and the policeman came to my window.

I just knew I was in trouble, but I didn't know what I did. I rolled my window down, was just about to say something in my defense, when he said, "Sir, I am sorry to disturb you, but I just had to stop you and thank you. We have been here a few hours and you are the first person that was actually doing the speed limit. In fact, you were doing 43 in a 45 zone."

"That's it?" I blurted out in relief.

"Yes, that's it. I just want to thank you again and encourage you keep driving safely. Have a great day."

I think I might have said a weak "OK" as I meandered back onto the road, my jaw hanging down in disbelief. And then I really started to think...

I wonder what type of emotions our Scouts have when they see us approach? Are they panicky like me? Do their little minds race trying to figure out what kind of trouble is heading their way? Are they feverishly trying to answer the question, "What did I do?" Gosh, I hope not.

I really don't want them to see any of us as the "Campout Police" but as a friend and mentor. But, how can we change our image to them?

It's simple; just excel at catching them doing something right! That's right, jump on them when they least expect it and praise them for something they just did. Don't wait for them to solve all of the world's problems to give them a pat on the back.

Thank them when they listen, or thank them when they show up on time. Do it especially if they are having trouble in that area. Do it the very next time you see them. Then do it again, and again, and again!!!

You see, we all learn much better when we are praised. We all know when we screw up, but many times we never realize we actually have our act together. A single word of praise here will crystallize the moment!

I try to keep a 10/1 or better compliment/criticism ratio. Sure, it's human nature to criticize, but go against that, and you will see your boys eager to have you around. More importantly, you will see their character flourish!

PETE MURRAY
Boy Scout Roundtable Commissioner, Central Florida Council

"Fla-Bob" Pete Murray is a Woodbadge Bobwhite and Eagle as well as an Assistant Scoutmaster.

Showing Courtesy

The following are some tips for showing Courtesy. Add your own in the blanks and check each one off as you do it.

❑ Be on time. Don't keep others waiting.

❑ Answer an invitation before the deadline.

❑ Hold the elevator for someone rushing to get on.

❑ Let a driver into your lane.

❑ Allow an elderly person to go ahead of you in line.

❑ Refrain from interrupting someone.

❑ Use your turn signals when driving your car or riding your bike.

❑ Look someone in the eye when talking with them and give them your undivided attention.

❑ Offer someone else the TV remote control.

❑ Say, "Excuse me" when you bump into someone, even if it wasn't your fault.

❑ Don't rush to be first when a new cashier opens up. Instead, point it out to the shopper next in line.

❑ Send a thank you card or e-mail.

❑ When driving, observe crosswalks and stay behind the line at red lights so pedestrians can cross freely.

❑ Let people exit a room or elevator before you try to enter.

❑ Adjust the driver's seat of your car to make it easier for your spouse.

❑ Admit a mistake and apologize.

❑ Say, "Goodbye" at the end of a phone conversation, don't just hang up.

❑ Park your car within the lines in a parking lot so that the people next to you can enter and exit their vehicle easily.

❑ Go with the flow when exiting a theater and don't push slower patrons.

❑ Have your money ready when you reach the cashier so you do not delay others behind you in line.

❑ Be polite. Say, "Please," "Thank you," and "You're welcome."

❑ Move out of the fast lane to let another car pass you.

❑ When you bring someone into a conversation or meeting, introduce them if they do not already know the other participants.

❑ Ask for something rather than demand it.

❑ Turn off your high beams when approaching another car.

❑ _____

❑ _____

❑ _____

❑ _____

❑ _____

He who sows courtesy reaps friendship, and he who plants kindness gathers love.

ST. BASIL

DAY 21

APPRECIATE NATURE

*Treasuring and enjoying the wonders of
our natural world.*

S couts love the outdoors. There are so many wonderful
things in nature to enjoy: stargazing at night; listening to
owls, frogs, and crickets; and admiring the dew on a spider's
web or a new bud on a plant.

Sometimes we get caught up in deadlines and schedules
but Appreciating Nature helps balance our lives. Standing
next to a 500 year-old redwood tree puts today's frustrations
into perspective. The ocean's calm waves that can turn,
overnight, into a raging fury with awesome force remind us
of the power and beauty of nature.

Every part of our country, every place in our world contains
marvelous elements of nature just waiting to be appreciated.
Scouts recognize that we are just caretakers of the land, for our
lifetimes are but dots on the timeline of the earth.

Former New Jersey Governor Christie Whitman learned
to Appreciate Nature as a young girl. Her dedication to
preserving it has led her to become our country's chief
protector of the outdoors, as Administrator of the
Environmental Protection Agency.

PROTECTING NATURE

As a child growing up on a farm in New Jersey, my father gave me instructions that remain with me to this day. He insisted that we always leave our environment cleaner than we found it.

This meant picking up a discarded wrapper in the woods, taking a bottle out of the stream when canoeing, and always making sure never to leave behind our own garbage.

I remember thinking that the rule was an easy one to follow, but given the amount of trash I picked up, it seemed few people did.

As my appreciation for the outdoors grew, my father's words became more than simple instructions. They provided a set of values for living, a code of ethics for enjoying the outdoors, and a standard to which you could help others aspire.

As head of the Environmental Protection Agency, these words have become a mission statement. I am just a temporary steward of this post, as we all are of our Earth, but my work is guided by the desire to leave our air cleaner, our water purer, and our land better protected than when I arrived.

For all lovers of the outdoors, these words sound familiar, and none more so than to Scouts. All outdoor Scouting activities are governed by this low impact mantra, but more important, the values which it represents are synonymous with Scouting. Courtesy, preparedness, and honor are qualities of good Scouts and good environmentalists.

So, when I see a Scout group "packing out" on a camping trip, clearing trails in the forest, or collecting litter on the highway, I realize that the "scouting way" is the way to a clean environment.

CHRISTIE WHITMAN
Administrator, Environmental Protection Agency

Christie Whitman has spent her career breaking down barriers. Prior to becoming Administrator of the EPA, she was New Jersey's first female Governor and appointed the state's first African-American State Supreme Court Justice, its first female State Supreme Court Chief Justice, and its first female Attorney General.

For additional information about
Christie Whitman, visit www.epa.gov/adminweb/about.htm.

APPRECIATE NATURE

Below are a few ideas for Appreciating Nature. Add your own in the blanks and check each one off as you try it.

❑ Take a walk around your neighborhood. Learn the names of at least 3 plants or trees.

❑ Make a bird feeder and find out the names of the species that visit.

❑ Put a live plant on your desk or in your window and bring a bit of nature indoors. Plants are beautiful, produce oxygen, and have a calming influence.

❑ Go for a long hike in a park or open area. Count the animals you see including those you see evidence of (such as footprints or feathers).

❑ Start an aquarium.

❑ Watch how gracefully animals move, then how they freeze and stand totally still. Walk softly, to get close to small animals and birds.

❑ Make a snowman (or woman).

❑ Use a compass to see which direction your home faces: North, South, East, or West.

❑ Visit a flower stand or nursery and smell the flowers.

❑ Splash around in rain puddles with your kids (or parents).

❑ Make sure you have bags when you walk your dog, and clean up after it.

❑ Find animal shapes in the clouds.

❑ Walk barefoot through the grass.

❑ When you are in a new area notice 3 ways in which nature is different there.

❑ Stargaze and learn some of the constellations in your area.

❑ Join an organization dedicated to protecting the environment such as the Sierra Club or Surfrider Foundation.

❑ Visit a national park.

❑ Use pump-spray dispensers rather than aerosol cans.

❑ In spring, clean the hair from your hairbrush and put it out for the birds to use for building their nests.

❑ _____

❑ _____

❑ _____

❑ _____

❑ _____

The best remedy for those who are afraid, lonely or unhappy is to go outside, somewhere where they can be quiet, alone with the heavens, nature and God.

Because only then does one feel that all is as it should be and that God wishes to see people happy, amidst the simple beauty of nature.

As long as this exists, and it certainly always will, I know that then there will always be comfort for every sorrow, whatever the circumstances may be. And I firmly believe that nature brings solace in all troubles.

ANNE FRANK

DAY 22

BE A GOOD SPORT

Accepting both winning and losing, graciously.
Playing fair and observing the rules.

S couts know that no one wins them all. Thus, they must learn how to deal with both success and failure, on the field and off.

This ability affects not only our success and enjoyment of life but also our relationships with other *players* such as our family, friends, teachers, co-workers, and bosses.

Part of being a good sport is acknowledging the contributions of others in our success. Quarterbacks need protection from their front lines, actors depend upon writers, salespeople rely on their customer support department, and successful Scout units require committed and trained youth and adult leaders.

Sometimes it is hard to remember that even established sports legends like Arnold Palmer were once just Scout age and how much their lives were shaped by their parents. It is a responsibility that we, as today's parents, must not ignore.

A Bittersweet Victory

Both my parents were on hand to watch my match in the West Penn Junior finals. Frustrated at having missed a short putt, I turned and threw my putter in disgust over the gallery and some small trees.

My elation at winning quickly vanished when I was greeted with dead stone silence in the family car. "If you ever throw a club like that again," my father told be, barely restraining his fury, "you'll never play in another golf tournament."

I remember what a long ride back to Latrobe it was. Thank God my mother was there, slipping me affectionate quiet glances to let me know how proud she was of me.

I know my father was brimming with pride as well, but I'd violated one of his cardinal rules about life and golf— that learning to be a gracious loser is at least as important as being a gracious winner. Being an ungracious winner was perhaps the worst thing he could imagine.

I was enough like my mother, I guess, that I was incapable of hiding my emotions at either winning or losing. But thanks to Pap, I learned the value of never publicly displaying my frustration—frustration every golfer experiences—and keeping my emotions in the bottle when I lost, regardless of the depth of the disappointment, of which there would be plenty.

More to the point, I never threw a club like that in anger again. At least not when my father was anywhere around to see it.

Arnold Palmer
Golfer

Arnold Palmer is a native of Latrobe, Pennsylvania. When he was just four his father, who worked at Latrobe Country Club, cut down a set of golf clubs to fit him and his lifelong love of golf began. An extremely popular player, Mr. Palmer was voted *Athlete of the Decade* and *Sports Illustrated's Sportsman of the Year*. Mr. Palmer now owns Latrobe Country Club, where he got his start. For additional information about Arnold Palmer, visit http://www.wsff.com/wsff/applications/Biographies/subdefault.asp? BiosID=1513&vCompId=49195&vSeqID=1.

PRACTICING SPORTSMANSHIP

Here are some drills for practicing Sportsmanship. Add your own in the blanks and check each one off as you exercise it.

❑ Play nice. Be fair and observe the rules, even when your opponents do not.

❑ Focus on enjoying the game not the end result. Remember, it's not whether you win or lose, it's how you play the game.

❑ Acknowledge a great play by your opponent. Then, learn it and add it to your repertoire.

❑ If you lose the competition, don't lose your temper along with it.

❑ If you win, don't get cocky. Be Humble, there are still losses in your future.

❑ In a loss, figure out the things the other side did better and practice them.

❑ Cheer for your team but don't boo the opposition, especially in youth sports.

❑ When the game (or other competition such as an election) is over—it's over. You can be fierce opponents on the field yet best friends off it.

❑ Call, write, or e-mail someone who helped you get to where you are today and tell them what their contribution has meant to you.

❑ Be a positive soccer (baseball, football, etc.) parent. Resist the temptation to challenge the coach or umpire's decisions, particularly in front of the players.

❑ Let go of a grudge against a former opponent. Leave the past in the past and work on the future.

❑ When you are outvoted, go along with the program and be a contributing member of the group.

❑ Don't pout when things are not going your way, be Cheerful.

❑ Thank your secretary, spouse, or other support people who help you every day.

❑ Be less concerned about being right and more concerned about achieving your and your team's goal.

❑ _____

❑ _____

❑ _____

❑ _____

❑ _____

It teaches the strong to know when they are weak and the brave to face themselves when they are afraid. To be proud and unbowed in defeat yet humble and gentle in victory.

And to master ourselves before we attempt to master others. And to learn to laugh, yet never forget how to weep. And to give the predominance of courage over timidity.

GENERAL DOUGLAS MACARTHUR

DAY 23

TEAMWORK

*Multiple individuals combining resources and
working together toward a common goal.
Placing the group's goal above team members'
personal goals. All for one and one for all!*

Working together as a Team, with a mutual goal, we can accomplish much more than as individuals with competing agendas. The key to a cohesive Team is the willingness of its members to subordinate their individual goals and egos to the Team.

Scouting is excellent training for Teamwork because Scouts get experience being both leaders and followers, planners and implementers. Successful Teams require Trust, good Leadership, and members Helping each other—all of which are elements of Scouting.

Scouts learn not to sit on the sidelines of life. When they see something that is wrong they become part of the solution. Teams aren't only in sports, being a Team player is an attitude for the game of life.

Although it is children who get the grades, parents play an important supporting role in education. It is our responsibility to make sure that they have a quiet place to work, the necessary tools (such as calculator, paper, and computer), and guidance to keep them on track.

Every Team member has their strengths and contributes in their own way. Some are better at offense than defense (or better at sales than technical support). Our task is to find the right position for ourselves and help our Teammates find theirs. Remember, Team spells:

Together **E**veryone **A**chieves **M**ore

One place we are sure to find Teamwork is at "The Happiest Place on Earth." In today's *Scouting Way* story, Disney CEO Michael Eisner reminisces about the origins of his Team spirit.

CAMP KEEWAYDIN

By far the most important formative experience in my life was going to Camp Keewaydin in Salisbury, Vermont.

The oldest wilderness camp in America, Keewaydin taught boys how to cook, pitch tents, portage canoes, "wallop" pans (meaning "clean" in Keewaydinese), and dry them with "elephant bumwad" (paper towels).

To this day, it remains Spartan, no-frills, and extremely low-tech. Campers live in tents, plumbing is minimal, and the only telephone is in the main office.

I went to Camp Keewaydin when I was eight and returned nearly every summer thereafter until I was twenty-two, the last few times as a staff member. All three of my sons followed in my footsteps.

To a remarkable degree, my core values were shaped in the crucible of those camp summers. Much like Scouts, Keewaydin focused on building practical skills and encouraging teamwork.

The highest virtues were helping the other fellow even as you learned the tools of self-reliance; being a good winner, but an even better loser; and learning to survive, gracefully and without complaint, under challenging conditions.

I learned a lot about leadership, teamwork and the simple congeniality of pulling together for a common goal.

MICHAEL EISNER
Chairman and CEO, The Walt Disney Company

Michael Eisner never saw a Disney film until he became a new father and saw *Pinocchio* with his son. However, as CEO of Disney for over 15 years, he has turned the niche company into one of the largest media conglomerates in the world and expanded Disney's influence into new frontiers.

A longtime advocate for kids and schools, Mr. Eisner created *Disney's American Teacher Awards*, "To honor teachers the same way we honor politicians and entertainers." For more details about Michael Eisner, visit http://lcweb.loc.gov/loc/lcib/9911/eisner.html.

TEAM SPIRIT

The following are ways to build Team spirit. Add your own in the blanks. Check each one off as you practice it.

❑ Work together on a family project, such as cleaning up the garage or washing the car, and make it fun.

❑ Organize a Neighborhood Watch rather than just complain about crime in your community.

❑ Pass the shot and assist in making the goal. Next time it may be your turn to score.

❑ Bag your own groceries when lines at the market are long. It helps everyone.

❑ When you're the leader, lead. When you are not, be a gracious Team player and work hard anyway.

❑ Let the whole family vote to decide a family outing or vacation.

❑ Rather than sitting on the sidelines giving orders to kids or subordinates, jump in and work alongside them.

❑ Help your family by putting something away at home that isn't your responsibility.

❑ Candidly assess where you can be most valuable to your Team and go there. Are you better at programming than writing marketing materials?

❑ Help a Teammate become stronger in their area, even if they compete with you for a position.

❑ Display a positive attitude to keep your Team motivated, even when you are feeling down.

❑ Praise your Team members.

❑ Do one of your child's chores for them when they are studying hard for school. School is a Team effort. Students on the front line need parents who support them. By lending a hand, you are both helping them succeed and showing them that their achievements are important to you.

❑ Be the *designated driver* for your group.

❑ Solicit ideas from everyone in your group, family, company, or Scout unit—and listen to them.

❑ Help each Team member find an area where they can be the leader.

❑ Schedule a company meeting offsite. New locations can spur new ideas.

❑ Acknowledge your receptionist, accountant, shipping person, and other Team members who keep your Team going but are frequently overlooked.

❑ When it's your turn to do an unpopular task, like cleanup, Do Your Best and do it Cheerfully.

❑ _____

❑ _____

❑ _____

❑ _____

The way a team plays as a whole determines its success. You may have the greatest bunch of individual stars in the world, but if they don't play together, the club won't be worth a dime.

BABE RUTH

DAY 24

HELPFUL

Offering assistance when it's not required and
without expecting to benefit, personally, from it.
Giving of yourself, rendering aid.

Helpful is more than a simple act or deed, it's an attitude. It requires the Kindness to care when people need help and the Perseverance to deliver the assistance.

Helpfulness permeates Scouting, from Giving Back to Your Community to Doing a Good Turn Daily to the Bravery required to help someone even when we are afraid.

Good deeds do not have to be big deeds. Sometimes it's the little things we do to help one another that really matter. Scouts remember to reach out to forgotten and neglected people, such as senior citizens and the homeless, who need our help.

It takes only a few moments but Helpfulness can make someone's day. What is simple for a tall person may be harder for a shorter one. Young muscles can dig and lift more easily than older ones.

Today's *Scouting Way* story from Scout leader Cheryl Baraty illustrates what happens when Helpfulness becomes ingrained in young adults.

SCOUT SPIRIT

O n behalf of Troop 392 of the Harry and Rose Sampson Family Jewish Community Center of Milwaukee, we are writing to support the Scout Spirit Award Nomination of Troop 194 chartered by the Abiding Savior Lutheran Church in Brown Deer, Wisconsin.

The Boy Scouts from that Troop who attended the 2001 Northeast District Winter Vista/Klondike demonstrated true Scout spirit and should be publicly recognized for their selfless acts.

Our Troop shared sleeping space with Troop 194 during the Klondike. Some of the boys from both Troops knew each other from school so conversation between the boys started easily, and all the boys discovered how much they had in common and liked each other. A nice time was enjoyed by all but we did not realize how much the interaction inspired the boys of Troop 194.

Saturday morning before all the Scouts went out on the trails the Scoutmaster of Troop 194 informed Winter Vista/Klondike Chair Dougie Reed that the boys of his Troop had decided that they wanted to use the nuggets they earned on the trail at the auction to bid on something that our Troop could use as they were a much more established Troop and had more equipment that we had. They had asked him to get permission from Dougie to do so. Dougie gave his blessing to such a selfless act.

At the auction, Troop 194 made sure to sit with our unit. As leaders we noticed lots of talking between the two groups but did not realize what was going on. Our boys wanted an item of which there were three. They were outbid on all three. The third time, the boys of Troop 194 bid on the item and won. They immediately presented the item to our Troop. Our boys immediately offered to bid on an item for their Troop. A detailed discussion among all the boys ensued and our unit was able to obtain an item for Troop 194 that they can use. All the boys left the auction the best of friends. We, the leaders of both units, just watched the entire process in awe.

For the record it should be noted that Troop 194 earned the award for the most nuggets earned on their trail. They also earned the most nuggets overall of all Troops attending the 2001 Winter Vista/Klondike. We at Troop 392 believe that their self-imposed incentive to work for the good of someone else inspired them to perform at or even above their best.

They are truly an example of how living the Scout spirit brings out the best in people and makes the world a better place to be. Their acts are even more admirable given that the Scouts chose their course of action on their own. Their adult leaders, Scoutmaster Dan Theine and Assistant Scoutmaster David Vandermolen, and all their parents should be secure in the knowledge that their leadership and guidance has truly been working in the manner envisioned by the Scouting Program.

These boys will truly be the leaders of tomorrow. Abiding Savior Lutheran Church has much to be proud of and we applaud their Scouting program's success with their youth.

It is not often that we as leaders get to see true Scout spirit in action. The selfless actions of the boys of Troop 194 were a real life lesson of how the values taught in Scouting can really improve the lives of youth and those around them. We in Troop 392 for the record want to express our appreciation not just for the gift of Troop 194, but much more importantly for the life lesson the boys of Troop 194 taught us.

We also want to point out that this was a wonderful interfaith experience for both Troops. Both units are chartered by a specific religious institutions, yet the boys of both troops managed to find the commonality of Scouting to reach out to each other. What a wonderful lesson for them to come away with! What a wonderful example of the Scouting program in action!!

Last, we want to thank the Milwaukee Boy Scout Council for allowing the Milwaukee Jewish Community Center to provide our Boy Scouts with the true meaning of reverence through Scouting activities.

As Jewish youth participating in Scout activities, our boys have learned to be proud of their heritage while learning about religions and cultures different from their own. We put on the Interfaith Service at the 2001 Northeast District Winter Vista/Klondike event as well as at the 2000 Northeast/Northwest District Fall Camporee, the latter including the Jewish Havdalah Service for the end of the Sabbath, which has given our boys the opportunity to learn to get up in front of large crowds and to publicly make presentations about things both familiar and unfamiliar to them. It has been a growing experience for our boys.

CHERYL P. BARATY
Boy Scout Troop Committee Chair, Milwaukee, WI

Cheryl Baraty is a Cubmaster and Chair of the
Milwaukee Jewish Committee on Scouting.

HELPING OUT

Here are a few tips for being Helpful. Add your own in the blanks. Today, look for opportunities to be Helpful and check them off.

❑ Do an extra chore around the house, such as folding laundry or putting away dishes, without being asked.

❑ Carry a bag or package for an elderly person struggling with it.

❑ Assist a co-worker with a tough project when it is not your responsibility to do so.

❑ Hold an elevator or other door open for someone.

❑ Use your knowledge to help a friend process or solve a problem.

❑ Pull out a shopping cart for the next person at a store.

❑ Tutor other students at your school.

❑ Volunteer at your child's school to work in the classroom, library, playground, or other area.

❑ Offer to drive your children and their friends somewhere fun.

❑ Back off and let another driver merge easily into traffic in front of you.

❑ Help another shopper get an item down from a high shelf in a store.

❑ Lend someone your cell phone to make a call so they don't have to go find a payphone.

❑ Help a child learn to ride a bicycle.

❑ When someone asks a question aloud, and you know the answer, tell them.

❑ Be a good assistant to someone who has come to help you out.

❑ If you are making a lot of copies and someone comes in who needs just a few, pause your job and let them work theirs in.

❑ Care enough to tell a friend something they do not want to hear—but really need to hear.

❑ Hold down a spring-loaded seat, such as in a movie theater, to make it easier for someone to sit down.

❑ Be there for someone who needs emotional support. Just listening can be Helpful.

❑ Turn something in to the Lost and Found.

❑ Put a divider before and after your groceries when checking out at the market.

❑ _____

❑ _____

❑ _____

❑ _____

❑ _____

*It is one of the most beautiful compensations of life,
that no man can sincerely try to help another
without helping himself.*

RALPH WALDO EMERSON

DAY 25

STRIVE FOR SUCCESS

*Setting high goals and devoting yourself
to achieving them.*

R eaching our goals requires a combination of many
Scouting values: the Vision to identify our objective and
create a plan, Preparedness to equip ourselves with the tools
we'll need, the commitment to Do Our Best, and the
Perseverance and Cheerfulness to keep at it until we succeed.

We must Strive for Success in all areas: family, friends,
work, financial, and self-satisfaction. Success is commonly
measured in terms of the car we drive or the house we live
in because those are quantifiable. But it is overall, balanced
success that produces happiness and satisfaction with life.

To be successful we need to manage our resources and
recognize that our actions directly affect the outcome.
Scouts know that goals are the stepping stones on the road
to success and the setbacks along the way are opportunities
to learn and grow. Success is a life journey.

The coach of Penn State's football team for over fifty years,
Joe Paterno offers sage advice about what it takes to win—
both on the field and off—in today's *Scouting Way* story.

STRIVING FOR SUCCESS

"A man's reach must exceed his grasp:
or what's a heaven for?"

ROBERT BROWNING

That Browning quotation has always been a favorite of mine. If everything worthwhile is within reach, what satisfaction is there in achievement?

Genuine satisfaction results from honest effort, often in the face of immense odds. Any athlete, indeed any ordinary citizen, gets a larger thrill from earning something than having it given to them. I've always told my players there is as much passion in the pursuit of excellence as there is in the achievement of excellence.

We establish exacting standards for ourselves on the athletic field. Eleven men must function as one. A player who operates independently can frustrate the goals of the team. Because football demands players act in harmony, I think success on the gridiron is especially satisfying.

Great individual efforts often turn the tide in college football but, acting alone, one athlete seldom produces victory. A great passer needs a receiver. A great kicker needs a holder and snapper. A gifted running back needs blockers. A Head Coach needs assistants.

Football is a great game, most of all, for the lessons it teaches. Players must learn to be disciplined. They must conform to the team concept. They must become familiar with pain and deal with the limits of their own endurance. They learn to play within the rules. They face the disappointment of failure and the sweetness of success.

These are all lessons which young people in the stands also need to learn as they move through life.

I've always preached to our players to have respect for their opponents. There is no victory so sweet as one over a formidable foe, an opponent who has tested our every resource before reluctantly bowing.

Most of all, football is about reaching—to become better as an individual, as a team, as a conference. And, as Browning said, the goals should require a healthy stretch. I always challenge our Penn State players to be the very best they can be. Twice that has been to the National Championship in 1982, and 1986.

Future Penn State teams may come up short of the No. 1 ranking. But, I fervently hope, no one will be able to criticize us for not reaching!

JOE PATERNO
Head Football Coach, Penn State University

Joe Paterno has coached the Penn State Nittany Lions for over 50 years and is still going. He has won more bowl games (19) than any coach in history and was honored as *Coach of the Year* an unprecedented four times.

Coach Paterno was the first football coach ever named *Sportsman of the Year* by *Sports Illustrated*. (The only other college coach, in any sport, so honored was UCLA basketball coach John Wooden. See Day 28, The Golden Rule.)

More than 200 of Coach Paterno's ex-Lions have gone on to play in the NFL. For more information about Coach JoePaterno, check out www.gopsusports.com/football/people/paterno/paternobiobody.cfm.

STRIVING FOR SUCCESS

Below are some excellent ways to Strive for Success. Add your own on the blank lines. Check off each one that you succeed in and put extra effort into everything you do today.

❑ Identify a goal, create a plan to achieve it, and put your plan into action.

❑ Appreciate a small success.

❑ Learn something new that will help you reach your goals or improve your life.

❑ Evaluate your strengths, objectively, and focus them on your success.

❑ Rehearse your presentation one more time or run an extra set of drills.

❑ Find a mentor.

❑ Enhance your skills by learning from a failure. Figure out what you did wrong and how to avoid it in the future.

❑ Re-examine your goals and raise at least one of them to a higher level.

❑ Figure out how to leverage one of your strengths to compensate for an area where you are weak.

❑ Reach out to someone in your group or team who you haven't gotten along with in the past.

❑ Maintain a Cheerful, positive attitude, no matter the circumstances.

❑ Read a motivational book and give one to friend to help them succeed, too.

❑ Subscribe to an inspirational e-mail newsletter such as *The Scouting Way* (www.ScoutingWay.com) or *Chicken Soup for the Soul* (www.ChickenSoup.com).

❑ Do Your Best, give 110% effort to a task.

❑ Focus on, and enjoy, an area where you are already successful.

❑ Check your gear and plan one more time. Think of everything that could go wrong and develop a back-up plan to Be Prepared.

❑ Talk to someone who is already successful in your field. Ask for pointers and be very appreciative.

❑ Candidly assess your weakest area and work on it, perhaps by taking a class or seminar.

❑ Turn off the TV and read.

❑ Think of a method or technique you've used that has not worked well and develop a new approach.

❑ _____

❑ _____

❑ _____

❑ _____

❑ _____

There are no secrets to success. It is the result of preparation, hard work, learning from failure.

U.S. SECRETARY OF STATE COLIN POWELL

DAY 26

HONOR

Respect, maintaining a good name or public esteem.
A reputation for integrity.

We Honor our country by serving it and flying the flag. We Honor our parents by showing them respect and treating them with dignity. We Honor someone who is no longer living with memories. Scouts live with Honor by being Honest, Brave, Trustworthy, and Accepting Responsibility for What They Say and Do.

To Honor ourselves requires self-esteem or self-worth, which we gain by believing that our decisions and actions are right and Honorable.

We maintain our Honor by accepting responsibility for our actions. If we follow Coach Lou Holtz's advice (Day 19) when making our decisions, our Honor will be safe.

Honor is at the core of Scouting both in values and in actions. Scouts live with Honor and use ceremonies and Reverence to Honor people and ideals.

In today's *Scouting Way* story, we hear about Honor from *Moses* himself, Charlton Heston.

HONOR

"Honor is a gift a man must give himself"

PATRICK HENRY

Honor is, I think, the rarest of all human virtues...yet perhaps the most valuable. The higher mammals share some qualities with Man: bravery, some skill at problem solving, protection of the young, and certainly loyalty. Harder to define though, and much harder to possess is honor.

Patrick Henry knew it in his heart. In the end, honor is a gift that can only be self-bestowed. Each man, in his heart's core, must give it to himself...if he dares. A gift only each individual one of us can validate.

CHARLTON HESTON
Actor
President, National Rifle Association

Charlton Heston is best known for his portrayal of *Moses* in Cecil B. DeMille's 1956 classic film, *The Ten Commandments*, and the 1959 film, *Ben-Hur*, for which he won an Academy Award.

Currently, Mr. Heston is President of the NRA. For more information about Charlton Heston, visit www.spleenworld.com/heston/.

LIVING WITH HONOR

Here are a few suggestions for living with Honor. Think of your own and add them in the blanks. Today, focus on making Honor an integral part of your life.

❑ Play by the rules—win or lose. Never cheat to win because you will have cheated yourself along with your opponent.

❑ Honor those who gave or risked their lives for your freedom by reading about them with your kids or marching in a parade.

❑ Dispose of a frayed flag properly, such as by giving it to a Scout unit, and get a new one.

❑ Call your parents (if you are fortunate enough that they are still alive). Honor them with the same time and commitment as they age, that they gave you growing up.

❑ Plan a ceremony to Honor something or someone important to you.

❑ Don't seek conflict but do not flee from it, either, if your principles or ideals are at stake.

❑ Honor your ancestors by tracing your family tree. A valuable resource is www.EllisIslandRecords.org.

❑ Accept a mistake, learn from it, and move on. Never look for a scapegoat.

❑ Visit your state or nation's capital and watch your system and elected representatives in action.

❑ Honor your commitment to meet a deadline even when you could get an extension.

❏ Plan a fun Mother's Day to Honor your mother or wife (be sure to include your children). Don't let her do any of the cooking or cleaning. And, remember your grandmother, if you are blessed by still having her alive.

❏ Honor your father or husband with a relaxing Father's Day. Have one of your kids mow the lawn or do another chore for him. Don't forget your grandfather, either, if you are lucky enough that he is still living.

❏ Visit a military cemetery on Memorial Day and appreciate the sacrifices made for your freedom.

❏ If something goes wrong with your product or service, stand behind it, no matter what.

❏ Do Your Best when Honoring your obligations. Don't just go through the motions.

❏ Ask your parents or grandparents to tell you about their war experience. Even if they did not serve in the military, they may have lived through rationing, lost friends or relatives, or collected material for the war effort.

❏ _____

❏ _____

❏ _____

❏ _____

❏ _____

Mine honour is my life; both grow in one.
Take honor from me, and my life is done.

WILLIAM SHAKESPEARE

DAY 27

DO YOUR BEST

*Trying as hard as you can. Giving something all
your effort, to the best of your abilities.*

Our best? What is that? When we are working with all
our heart and soul and mind, with all the strength and
talent we possess, then we're Doing our Best.

Scouts epitomize this principle. With their *Can Do*
attitude they give 110% effort, and their work ethic carries
over into their families, careers, and other organizations.
They always put their best foot forward and give everything
just a little extra effort. And, not just some times—but all
the time.

Doing Our Best means editing a report or practicing a
presentation one more time and paying extra attention to
the details. It means Continuing to Learn so we keep up
with advancements in our field and our best gets better.
Whatever we do for a living, we can make it our masterpiece. And like Scouts, everything we do we should do with
Cheerfulness and a positive attitude.

The commitment to Do Our Best stays with us long after
our Scouting years, as Oklahoma Governor Frank Keating
relates in his *Scouting Way* story.

DOING MY BEST

When I joined Troop 20 in Tulsa, Oklahoma, as an 11-year-old Tenderfoot, I had no background in Cubbing. Scouting was brand new to me—and it so happened that that year, Troop 20 was a young group, with many new Scouts. At one of the very first meetings, I was elected patrol leader! A Tenderfoot patrol leader!

That's how Scouting taught me its very first lesson: if I was going to succeed, I would need to apply the principles of the Scout Oath and Law (which I had only recently memorized) to a very large challenge.

I soon learned that no matter how much experience I might have or lack, I could contribute, and I could learn to be a leader. If I didn't know quite how to be Helpful to my patrol, I could open my ears and learn. If I wasn't too Brave about leading the patrol on that first campout, I might as well be Cheerful about it. I was determined to *Do My Best*.

Things worked out and I eventually achieved Star rank. That year, my mother became quite ill, and my father sent my twin brother and me to a boarding school for several months.

During my time away from the troop, as many young men do, I got interested in other things, and I dropped out of Scouting shy of Eagle. That, too, taught me a lesson—it was a bad decision I have regretted for many years.

Scouting taught me first to work and succeed, and second to examine my decisions carefully, since I might come to regret them later. Not a bad pair of messages for life.

FRANK KEATING
Governor of Oklahoma

Frank Keating began his career with the FBI, then moved on to Oklahoma's state House and Senate. Prior to becoming Governor, he held positions in the Treasury, Department of Justice, and Housing and Urban Development. For more information about Governor Frank Keating, visit www.governor.state.ok.us/govbio.htm.

DOING YOUR BEST

Below are several ways to Do Your Best plus room to add your own, specific to your work or lifestyle. As you go through your day, look for opportunities to Do Your Best and check them off.

❑ Be on time.

❑ Add a splash of color or garnish to your cooking to enhance the presentation.

❑ When doing your schoolwork or setting the table for dinner take pride in your work and Do Your Best.

❑ Be the best parent by doing something special for your child (it doesn't have to be big, just spending time with them can be special).

❑ Be the best child by doing something special for your parents (even a simple phone call can make their day).

❑ Don't skip out early at school or work, even if no one will notice.

❑ Dress clean and neat, appearances matter.

❑ Find an error in your work that no one else would notice—and fix it anyway.

❑ Take a class, read a book, or get a tutor to help you improve in an area where you are Doing Your Best but still struggling.

❑ Give people your full attention when they are talking to you.

❑ Rehearse your presentation one more time.

❑ Express yourself clearly and say, "Yes" instead of "Yeah."

❑ Run an extra lap, shoot 10 more free throws, or practice another skill a little more than you normally would.

❑ Improve your posture; stand straight.

❑ Research a topic you are interested in but don't feel you have all the *best* information. Go to the library or try www.Google.com or www.AskJeeves.com on the Internet.

❑ Do more than the minimum requirement.

❑ If you are Doing Your Best but still aren't doing very well, be proud of yourself anyway. With continued effort you will improve, so don't give up.

❑ _____

❑ _____

❑ _____

❑ _____

❑ _____

If a man is called to be a street sweeper, he should sweep streets even as Michelangelo painted or Beethoven composed music or Shakespeare wrote poetry.

He should sweep streets so well that all the hosts of heaven and earth will pause to say, "Here lived a great street sweeper who did his job well."

DR. MARTIN LUTHER KING, JR.

DAY 28

THE GOLDEN RULE

Treat people as you would like to be treated.

The Golden Rule is the foundation for all Scouting values. Would we like people to be Friendly, Helpful, Honest, and Loyal to us? Of course, we would. Then, we must give those same considerations to others.

The Golden Rule is simple yet can guide us in all our actions and decisions. By asking ourselves how we would like the situation handled, if circumstances were reversed, we know what to do.

Taught by almost every religion including Christianity, Judaism, Buddhism, Islam, Hinduism, Taoism, and Confucianism, The Golden Rule is perhaps the world's most universally accepted ethical tenet.

In today's *Scouting Way* lesson, legendary UCLA basketball coach John Wooden shares the rules which have guided him throughout his life.

LIVING BY THE GOLDEN RULE

When I graduated from a small three-room country grade school, my father gave me a little card with the admonition, "Son, try to live up to these."

On one side was the following seven point creed:

Be true to yourself.

Help others.

Make each day your masterpiece.

Drink deeply from good books, especially the Bible.

Make friendship a fine art.

Build a shelter against a rainy day.

Give thanks for your blessings and pray for guidance everyday.

On the other side of the card was the following verse —

Four things a man must learn to do

If He would make his life more true;

To think without confusion—clearly,

To love his fellow man—sincerely,

To act from honest motives—purely,

To trust in God and Heaven—securely.

I wish I could say that I have lived up to this, but, being imperfect, I can't, but I can say that I have tried.

JOHN WOODEN
Author
Former UCLA Basketball Coach

John Wooden is well-known as the most successful coach in college basketball history. Under his leadership, the Bruins set all-time records with four perfect 30-0 seasons, 88 consecutive wins, 20 PAC 10 championships, and 10 national championships, including seven in a row. Coach Wooden is one of only 2 college coaches honored as *Sports Illustrated's Sportsman of the Year*. (The other is Penn State Coach Joe Paterno. See Day 25, Strive for Success.)

Less well-known is that Mr. Wooden was a phenomenal player: a three-time All-American and *College Player of the Year* in 1932. He is one of only two individuals enshrined in the Basketball Hall of Fame both as a player and as a coach. For details of Coach John Wooden's career, go to www.hoophall.com/halloffamers/Wooden.htm.

OBEYING THE GOLDEN RULE

Here are some ideas for obeying The Golden Rule. Add others as you think of them and check each one off as you apply it.

❏ Treat someone with extra respect and Kindness.

❏ When a person drops something, pick it up and hand it to them or let them know that they dropped it.

❏ Be polite to people and use a nice tone of voice in speaking with them.

❏ Call a friend you have been thinking about, don't wait for them to call.

❏ Treat your subordinates the way you want to be treated by your boss.

❏ Think of the social trait that annoys you most (such as interrupting or invading your personal space) and make a conscious effort not to do it to others.

❏ Remember something your parents did that made you feel loved and do it to your kids.

❏ Remember what your parents did that drove you crazy and don't do it to your children.

❏ Call attention to the contributions of others, such as Scout Leaders or your spouse, to gain them the recognition you want for your efforts.

❏ Treat a salesperson or restaurant server the way you would like customers to treat you, if that were your job.

❏ Say, "Please," "Thank you," and "You're welcome."

❑ Resist the temptation to tailgate the car ahead of you. It is not safe and won't get you to your destination any faster.

❑ When you arrive late to a class or meeting, enter as quietly and unobtrusively as possible and don't interrupt.

❑ Tell the truth.

❑ _____

❑ _____

❑ _____

❑ _____

❑ _____

GOLDEN RULES FOR LIVING

If you open it, close it.
If you turn it on, turn it off.
If you unlock it, lock it up.
If you break it, admit it.
If you can't fix it, call in someone who can.
If you borrow it, return it.
If you value it, take care of it.
If you make a mess, clean it up.
If you move it, put it back.
If it belongs to someone else and you want to use it,
get permission.
If you don't know how to operate it, leave it alone.
If it's none of your business, don't ask questions.
If it ain't broke, don't fix it.
If it will brighten someone's day, say it.
If it will tarnish someone's reputation, keep it to yourself.

MIRIAM HAMILTON KEARE

DAY 29

REVERENT

---

*A feeling of deep respect, mixed with wonder, fear
and love. A sense of awe. To Honor greatly.*

Reverence for God and his creations are an important
part of Scouting. We can be Reverent inside a building,
such as a church or temple, or outside in the mountains or
deserts. God—and the awesome power of the universe—is
everywhere.

Positive images, like the Grand Canyon and stars in the
night sky, can induce Reverence. As can negative ones, such as
the smoldering wreckage of the World Trade Center towers.

Less spectacular, but no less deserving of Reverence are
weddings, newborn babies, the opening of a rose, and Boy
Scout Eagle and Girl Scout Gold Award ceremonies.

In addition to embracing our own religion and traditions,
Reverence charges us with respecting the customs and
beliefs of others, as U.S. Secretary of Veteran Affairs and
Distinguished Eagle Scout Togo West, Jr. explains in today's
Scouting Way narrative.

WHAT SCOUTING MEANS TO ME

I well remember the impact Scouting had on me as a young boy. I grew up in Winston-Salem, North Carolina, and belonged to the Old Hickory Council. I have many good memories of that time—a time when I first set my feet on the path I have walked throughout my life.

One summer, our group of young Scouts boarded a diesel repair ship that belonged to the United States Navy. It wasn't much of a ship, but in our imagination it was as glorious as an aircraft carrier, or the largest battle cruiser in the fleet. We had a wonderful week sailing on that ship.

We were supposed to go south to Cuba, but a bearded revolutionary had just emerged from the Cuban hills, and forced us to change our plans. Instead, the Navy took us to Halifax, Nova Scotia—which for us was just as great an adventure.

I remember many times when we camped out in the cold and the wet. I clearly recall the fires we couldn't get to start despite all of our training; the carefully tended and cooked food that always tasted somewhat raw; and all the merit badges, like knot-tying, plant identification, and first aid, we labored so hard to earn.

And I remember, as all Scouts do, memorizing the twelve points of the Scout Law, and reciting them with my fellow Scouts. My trick was to learn how to say them as quickly as possible so they sounded like one word, and one law, so no one could tell that there was a possibility I might have missed one along the way. Now that I have met Scouts from all around the country, I found that I wasn't the only one who had hit upon this particular strategy.

When you recite the twelve points that way, though, something unusual happens. You get the sense of the Scout Law as a kind of unified whole, and a road map for life. As an adult, I concluded that that unified whole, instead of the dividing into twelve parts, actually divides more easily into three parts—three partnerships, or contracts, that a Scout makes for life.

The first of these partnerships or contracts are those that Scouts enter into with those around them—their families, parents, friends, neighbors, and their country. These are represented by the first seven provisions of the Scout Law, which state that a Boy Scout is trustworthy, loyal, helpful, friendly, courteous, kind and obedient. They are all about the way we treat others, and are a part of the Golden Rule: that in our attitude towards our country and our community we will do unto them as we hope that others will do unto us.

The second partnership extends through the eleventh provision: a Scout is cheerful, thrifty, brave and clean. This is a partnership Scouts make with themselves: how they will behave, what they expect of themselves, and what they will do in the future.

And the third partnership, which requires a Scout to be reverent, is the contract Scouts make with God or with whatever their family and their tradition have taught them is the supreme power. I would add that reverence, in this context, is not just reverence for our own personal view of the Supreme Being, but also our tolerance for the beliefs of others.

Over and over, in my daily life, I hear the principles of the Scout Law and the Scout Oath repeated by men and women of great learning and knowledge, proving their value in the everyday business of living. Those of us who have been Scouts hold Scouting close to our hearts. It has helped us to grow up along the right path, and to live lives of honor and commitment.

Today's generation needs Scouting as much, if not more, as any generation that has come before. So many negative forces vie with Scouting for a young person's time, and so many young people are attracted to those forces.

Scouting is not a program designed to take boys into the woods to camp and hike: it is a program designed to prepare them to take their places in today's competitive and increasingly changing American society. It has had a profound effect on my life, and on the lives of so many others. I am grateful for everything Scouting has taught me. Our country is grateful for what Scouting has taught millions of its finest citizens.

THE HONORABLE TOGO D. WEST, JR.
U.S. Secretary of Veteran Affairs
Distinguished Eagle Scout

Togo D. West, Jr. has served his country as Associate Deputy Attorney General in the Justice Department, General Counsel for the Navy, Special Assistant to the Secretary of Defense, General Counsel of the Department of Defense, and Secretary of the Army.

An Eagle Scout with Bronze Palm, Secretary West was named Distinguished Eagle Scout by the Boy Scouts of America. As Secretary of Veterans Affairs, he directs the federal government's second largest department. For more information about Secretary Togo West, see www.va.gov/biographies/west.htm.

A Reverence for Living

Below are a few suggestions for living with Reverence. Add your own as you think of them. Check them off as you follow them.

❑ Let an infant hold your finger and make eye contact with you.

❑ Learn about another religion or culture.

❑ Thank God for your blessings.

❑ Sit quietly and appreciate a sunrise or sunset.

❑ Earn a Scout Religious Emblem or serve as the Chaplain for your unit.

❑ Attend an Boy Scout Eagle Court of Honor or Girl Scout Gold Award Ceremony.

❑ Talk to your children about religion. Encourage their questions and answer them Honestly. Discover the answer you don't know, together.

❑ Respect your parents (whatever your age). They have earned it.

❑ Respect your children (whatever their age). Treat them as young adults.

❑ Take a walk in a park or woodland and enjoy the flowers and creatures.

❑ Remember your sense of wonder the first time you held a newborn baby.

❑ Walk along the ocean's edge and feel the waves lapping at your feet.

❑ Be flexible with your employees, allowing them time off to participate in their religious holidays.

❑ Meditate.

❑ Respect someone else's religious customs.

❑ Avoid killing living things when you are out in nature. It is their home, you are just visiting.

❑ Pray.

❑ Consider the ethical positions of companies as part of your investment criteria.

❑ Visit the mountains or desert.

❑ Attend a religious service.

❑ Refuse to let political correctness keep your organization from celebrating and enjoying a variety of religious holidays.

❑ Think of 3 things you Revere.

❑ _____

❑ _____

❑ _____

❑ _____

❑ _____

We have not the reverent feeling for the rainbow that a savage has, because we know how it is made. We have lost as much as we gained by prying into that matter.

MARK TWAIN

DAY 30

GRATITUDE

*An expression of appreciation. Realization and
acknowledgement of the help and gifts we receive.*

Scouts know that Gratitude is more than just a
Courteous, automatic, "Thank you." It is taking the time
and effort to truly appreciate what has been done for us,
then to communicate that appreciation to our benefactors.

When we Live Today, Appreciate Nature, and are
Cheerful we realize how much we have to be thankful for
and, in addition to God, how many people we have to thank.

So, it is appropriate that our last stop on *The Scouting Way*
is Gratitude. Nobody makes it all on their own. Not in a
family, company, sports team, or Scout unit. Our co-workers,
friends, teachers, family, and Scout leaders contribute more
to our success than we realize. We should be Grateful for
their contribution.

We owe a special thanks to the 30 inspirational leaders who
have guided us, this past month, along *The Scouting Way.*

Unfortunately, sometimes we take people for granted
and fail to realize their importance until they are gone, as
Scouter Leo Teunissen relates in the final *Scouting Way*
story. We must Do Our Best to ensure that does not happen.

THE PROMISE

It was in October of 2000 when this old man came into my auto parts store looking for a replacement part for his very old motor home.

Well, the only other one like it would be in the Smithsonian. So, I took a little super-glue and epoxy and fixed his old part, a little Boy Scout handyman work.

Then, while he was paying for the supplies I used, that's when it all happened. He looked over my shoulder, pointed, and asked with an old rough voice, "Is that a Boy Scout shirt I see hanging there?"

I looked over my shoulder into my office and said, "Yes, I just got it back from the cleaners."

"Are you a Boy Scout leader?" he asked.

"Well, yes I am. I have a troop here, right up the road," I said.

Then he asked, "Can I ask you a few questions about that?"

"Sure!" I said, thinking what's this all about?

He asked, "Do you still have meetings every week, where the boys learn their skills, like knot tying, knife and ax, and fire building?"

"Yes we do. Ours are on Monday nights," I said and added, "Knot tying and fire building are still some of the first things a Scout gets to learn."

"How about outings? Do you guys still do that, you know, go on hikes and campouts?" he asked.

I said, "Sure we do, at least once a month, sometimes more." Then I went on to explain some of what our troop had done and where we were going next.

He then said, "I was in Boys Scouts! That was a long time ago, during the Great Depression. It was real hard to be a Scout then. We didn't have any money to buy food, let alone a Scout uniform. So our Scoutmaster let us wear what we could. I wore an old work shirt of my Dad's. I would sew all our patches that we earned on that old shirt and boy! It looked real sharp! Do you still earn patches like that?" he asked.

"We sure do!" I said.

"You know we had a meeting every week, learned new skills and things. On the weekend, once a month, our Scoutmaster would take us for a hike. We would go out in the forest somewhere he had planned out. We boys would set up camp and get a big fire going. That was our job. Then that old Scoutmaster would pull out some hot dogs. Where or how he was able to get those, I don't know, but all us boys would roast them over our fire. Oh, they tasted so good!" he said. I could almost taste them myself. By now I noticed the old guy was red in the eyes.

He went on and said, "Those were great times. I had to leave Scouts because my family had to move. I lost contact with that Scoutmaster after that. Then came WWII and I went to fight the Japanese on some island." He didn't tell me the name of it or exactly what had happened.

But he said, "A few of my buddies and I were trapped by ourselves on that island, for a little more than a week. It was because of my Scout skills that all of us survived. They asked me how I learned to do those skills and I told them it was my old Scoutmaster that had taken the time to teach me. We all agreed that if we made it back, I would have to go and thank him for saving our lives and I promised I would."

Then he said, "Well, when I did come home, the first chance I had, I went to see him and tell him thanks. But when I got there I found his mother and she told me that he, too, had gone to war, only he went to Europe. He was one of the first to land on the beaches of Normandy."

Then with tears in his eyes, he said, "You know, he died a hero there!" He paused for a moment then said, "I never got a chance to thank him for saving our lives. I'd like it if I could to thank you, for him, for all of us?" he asked. I was speechless and all I could do was shake my head yes.

As I put my hand out to shake, he took my hand and pulled me in close to give me a hug. I could hear him cry as he said, "Thanks, from all the guys." Then he whispered, "You keep helping all those boys like you do. They don't know it, but they need you more now then I did then."

Letting go, he turned and started to walk for the door, then he stopped, turned around and pointed his old finger toward me. Then, with tears in his eyes he said, "You know! I'm 84 years old, my wife died eight years ago. It's because of Scouting that I've been camping ever since. Those years as a Scout were the best years of my life!"

I've not see him since that day. But, I will remember him all my life!

LEO TEUNISSEN
Scoutmaster, Mission Viejo, CA

Leo Teunissen has been a Scout leader for 12 years.
His son, Jon, is an Eagle Scout.

THANK YOU

Here are some tips for expressing Gratitude and space to write in your own. Check each one off as you convey it.

❑ Call your parents and say, "Thank you" for a happy moment you remember from childhood.

❑ Thank someone who offered you guidance raising your children.

❑ Tell the author of one of *The Scouting Way* stories what their words meant to you and how they helped you. E-mail it to thanks@ScoutingWay.com or mail it to The Scouting Way, PO Box 73302, San Clemente, CA 92673-0111 and we will forward it to them.

❑ At holiday times, give plates of cookies to all the service people (including doctors, teachers, dentists, mail carriers, sanitation workers, and school administrators) who help you throughout the year.

❑ Visit a school where you or your children attended and say, "Thank you" to a special teacher.

❑ Thank your mentor.

❑ Organize a way for the Scouts in your unit to show their appreciation to the adult leaders.

❑ Say, "Thank you" to your spouse and children for the chores they do.

❑ Send a thank you note to someone who did a Good Turn and helped you.

❑ Say a hearty, "Thank you" to everyone who gives you service including salespeople, bus drivers, and cashiers.

❑ Write a letter to a company praising an employee who was particularly Helpful to you.

❑ Show your appreciation for the people who support you at work.

❑ Really mean it when you say, "Thank you."

❑ Let your elected officials know you appreciate it when they vote the way you want them to.

❑ Show your gratitude to your children's teachers by giving them something for their classroom, like a set of whiteboard markers or Kleenex.

❑ Start a family Thanksgiving tradition, such as going around the table and having each person say what they are thankful for.

❑ Thank God for the world and show your Gratitude by Making the World a Better Place.

❑ _____

❑ _____

❑ _____

❑ _____

❑ _____

To speak gratitude is courteous and pleasant, to enact gratitude is generous and noble, but to live gratitude is to touch Heaven.

JOHANNES GAERTNER

THE TRAIL AHEAD

I n the beginning, Scouts follow their leaders, learn from them and other Scouts, and develop their skills. Ultimately, they blaze their own trail.

Over the past 30 days, we've traveled a long way together on *The Scouting Way*. Like in Scouting, we've learned a lot, had fun, and feel a sense of accomplishment at our growth.

Now it is time for each of us to strike out on our own—to mentor others as our 30 special leaders have done for us, as we continue to live *The Scouting Way*. But, just as the Scoutmaster is always there in the background to lend a hand, *The Scouting Way* will always be there to support you.

If you are not already a subscriber, we encourage you to sign up for the free *Scouting Way* newsletter and give free subscriptions to family, friends, and fellow Scouts at www.ScoutingWay.com.

We are currently collecting stories for the newsletter and a second *Scouting Way* book. If you have an inspirational story to share or the stories in this book have helped you in some way, please e-mail us at story@ScoutingWay.com or mail us at The Scouting Way, PO Box 73302, San Clemente, CA 92673-0111.

We look forward to further travels with you along *The Scouting Way*.

Yours in Scouting

SANDRA AND JEFF SCHWARTZ

BADEN-POWELL'S LAST MESSAGE

After Lord Baden Powell's death, in 1941,
this message was discovered amongst his writings.

Dear Scouts — If you have ever seen the play "Peter Pan," you will remember how the pirate chief was always making his dying speech because he was afraid that possibly when the time came for him to die he might not have time to get it off his chest. It is much the same with me, and so, although I am not at this moment dying, I shall be doing so one of these days and I want to send you a parting word of goodbye.

Remember, it is the last time you will ever hear from me, so think it over.

I have had a most happy life and I want each one of you to have a happy life too.

I believe that God put us in this jolly world to be happy and enjoy life. Happiness doesn't come from being rich, nor merely being successful in your career, nor by self-indulgence. One step towards happiness is to make yourself healthy and strong while you are a boy, so that you can be useful and so can enjoy life when you are a man.

But the real way to get happiness is by giving out happiness to other people. Try and leave this world a little better than you found it, and when your turn comes to die you can die happy in feeling that at any rate you have not wasted your time but have done your best.

"Be Prepared" in this way, to live happy and to die happy—stick to your Scout promise always—even after you have ceased to be a boy—and God help you to do it.

Your friend,

Baden-Powell of Gilwell

ABOUT THE AUTHORS

S andra and Jeff Schwartz are Scouting enthusiasts and leaders.

Sandra was a Brownie who went on through Cadettes. She led their daughter, Lauren's, Girl Scout troop from Daisies through Cadettes and is also a trained Boy Scout Leader who was very active in their son, Greg's, troop.

Jeff was a Cub Scout, himself, and Committee Chairman of Greg's Boy Scout troop for five years. He is a trained adult leader and a Woodbadge "Raven."

Sandra, Jeff and Lauren, along with Scout, their Labrador Retriever, live in San Clemente, California. Greg, an Eagle Scout, attends the University of California at Irvine.

In addition to Scouting, the Schwartz's have a passion for technology. They have been profiled and called "the ultimate wired family" and "real-life Jetsons" in publications including *The Wall Street Journal*.

They were also featured in a documentary video about *The Family of the Future*. The articles and video are available on *The Scouting Way* website (www.ScoutingWay.com) by clicking *About*.

The whole Schwartz family is collaborating on *The Guidebook for the Digital Family*, a book to help families integrate technology into their lives with positive results.